An
American
MOSAIC
Presented To:
Photo by Diane Kirkland

Photo by Bruce R. Feeley

An
American
MOSAIC
A Photographic Portrait of
Fayetteville and Cumberland County

If it's fall it has to be football season in the South. When the Methodist University Monarchs take to the field, tailgate parties, half-time shows, homecoming games, and cheering crowds are sure to be close behind. As part of the forty-four-year-old USA South Athletic Conference—whose headquarters is located in Fayetteville—the team has an impressive string of homecoming victories. Methodist University, which was founded in 1955, is a vital part of the Fayetteville community not only during football season, but throughout the year. ⋆

An
American
MOSAIC

EDITOR . . . . Rob Levin

PUBLISHER . . . . Barry Levin

ASSOCIATE PUBLISHER . . . . John Lorenzo

COMMUNITY LIAISON . . . . Kristie Lozano

CHIEF OPERATING OFFICER . . . . Renée Peyton

DESIGN MANAGER . . . . Ann Fowler

ASSOCIATE EDITOR . . . . Rena Distasio

PROJECT DIRECTOR . . . . Cheryl Sadler

PHOTO EDITORS . . . . Jill Dible, Ann Fowler

WRITERS . . . . Kimberly DeMeza, Rena Distasio,
. . . . Grace Hawthorne, Amy Meadows, Regina Roths, Gail Snyder

COPY EDITOR . . . . Bob Land

BOOK DESIGN . . . . Compōz Design

JACKET DESIGN . . . . Kevin Smith

PREPRESS . . . . Vickie Berdanis

PHOTOGRAPHERS . . . . Erin Brethauer, Bruce Feeley, Greg Foster,
. . Diane Kirkland, John Chang McCurdy, Rod Reilly, Alan S. Weiner

Published by Riverbend Books
an Imprint of Bookhouse Group, Inc.
818 Marietta Street, NW
Atlanta, Georgia 30318
www.riverbendbooks.net
404.885.9515

An American Mosaic : A Photographic Portrait of Fayetteville and Cumberland County /
[Rob Levin, editor].
p. cm. ISBN 978-1-883987-33-6
1. Fayetteville (N.C.)—Pictorial works. 2. Cumberland County (N.C.)—Pictorial works.
3. Fayetteville (N.C.)—Description and travel. 4. Fayetteville (N.C.)—Economic conditions.
5. Business enterprises—North Carolina—Fayetteville. I. Levin, Rob, 1955-
F264.F28A44 2007
975.6'373—dc22
2007036848

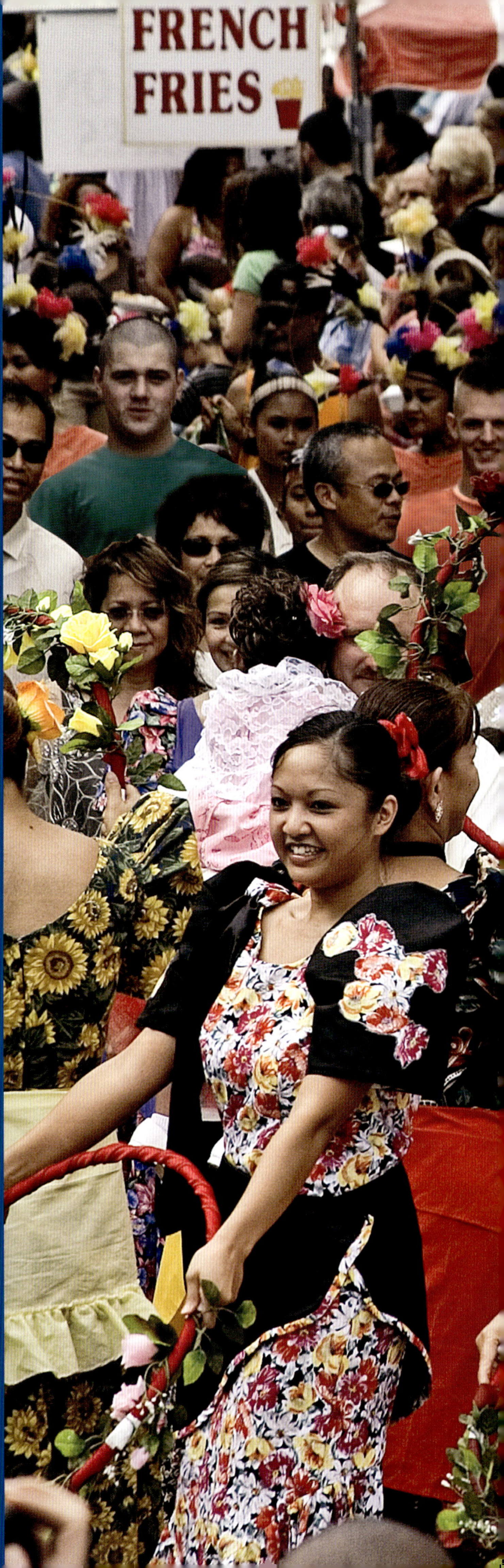

Fayetteville's multiple festivals provide a world of year-round entertainment, from gatherings that celebrate cultural diversity such as the International Folk Festival, to those that honor the brewer's art or occasions that combine a wine-tasting with music. Historic Hauntings, Fourth Friday arts displays, Craftmen's Christmas Festivals, and more: the fun fest is limitless, so put on your party hat, grab your shopping shoes, and come to Fayetteville! ★

Foreword 11

Live 18

Work 112

Play 178

Contents

Photo by Greg Foster

Photo by K. Kassens

*A*t Evans Metropolitan African Methodist Episcopal Zion Church, families come together to share in Sunday worship. The church fulfills its mission to be "a place of worship, a haven, and an inspiration to all" by bringing people together for Sunday services, weekly activities, and other events throughout the year. ★

Foreword

On behalf of the Cumberland County Business Council Board of Directors and the Business Council staff, I am delighted to present this photographic portrait of the Fayetteville area.

Cumberland County is home to over three hundred thousand people from all walks of life. Our close proximity to Fort Bragg and Pope Air Force Base brings so many people to our community from places around the world. Their presence enriches our area and brings an international flavor to our community that shows in our variety of restaurants, cultures, and neighborhoods.

The annual International Folk Festival offers smells and tastes from all over the globe. Local art thrives at street fairs and at the celebrated Dogwood Festival. Museums boast the history of the Cape Fear River and the accomplishments and trials of our Airborne and Special Operations units.

This mosaic of cultures and people makes Fayetteville the All-American City that it is today. With the revitalization of our downtown and the creation of economic development engines such as the Defense and Security Technology Accelerator and North Carolina Military Business Center, we are creating new opportunities that combine entrepreneurial spirit while fostering our military expertise.

In order to nurture the growth of our great community, the Business Council has advocated the business position, creating a climate of growth and success that benefits all. We provide a shared commitment to quality of life for everybody through sustaining local business and recruiting new industry to Cumberland County.

On behalf of the Cumberland County Business Council, it is an honor to show how Cumberland County's citizens, geography, patriotism, and historical significance create an unmatched community of diversity and hometown pride.

Gordon Rose
Chair 2007–2008

Photo by John Chang McCurdy

When the weather cools and the ducks and geese start their journeys southward, Tom Morketter goes to work, although in his case, work is really more like play. A native of Cumberland County, lifelong outdoorsman, and partner in Fayetteville's Tarheel Fish and Game Inc. outfitter and guide service, Tom specializes in leading clients on the kinds of trips that make memories for a lifetime. Today, he and his trusty Labrador retriever, Rocky, have set out to a local impoundment to scout for ducks. The secret to a good hunt other than a really good dog? "Do your homework," says Morketter. "You have to be where the waterfowl want to be." In the region, that could include private impoundments, reservoirs like Shearon Harris and Jordan Lakes, or spots along the Cape Fear River. Morketter also recommends off-season practice at a skeet shooting range to develop perfect aim for a clean shot. ✷

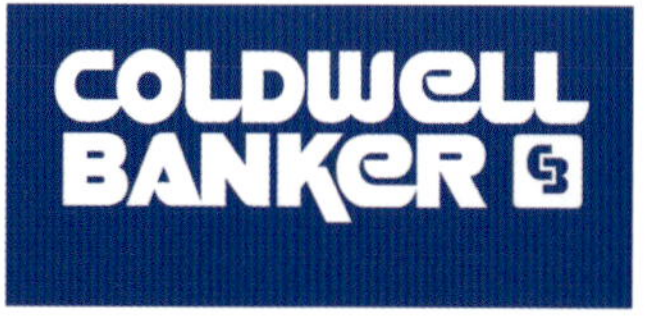

would not have been possible without the support of the following sponsors:

Cape Fear Valley Health System
City of Fayetteville
Fayetteville Regional Airport
Coldwell Banker United Realty
County of Cumberland
Courtyard by Marriott Fayetteville
Crown Center
Cumberland County Schools
Elmwood Partners, LLC
ERA Pennink & Strother Real Estate
Fayetteville State University
H&H Homes
Holiday Inn Bordeaux
Holmes Electric Security Systems
Hutchens, Senter & Britton, P.A.
Lafayette Ford
Partnership for Children of Cumberland County
Public Works Commission
Smith Barney

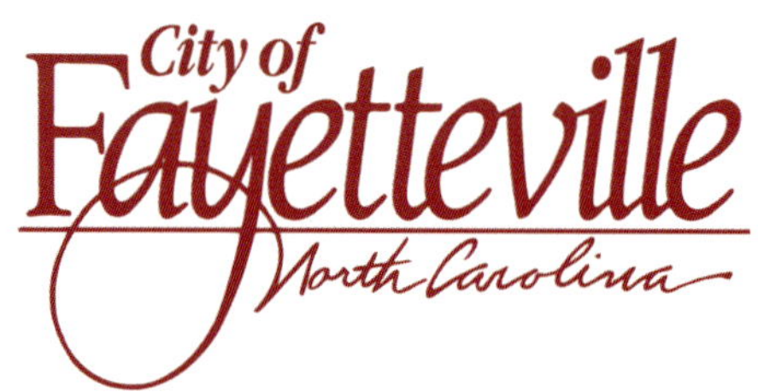

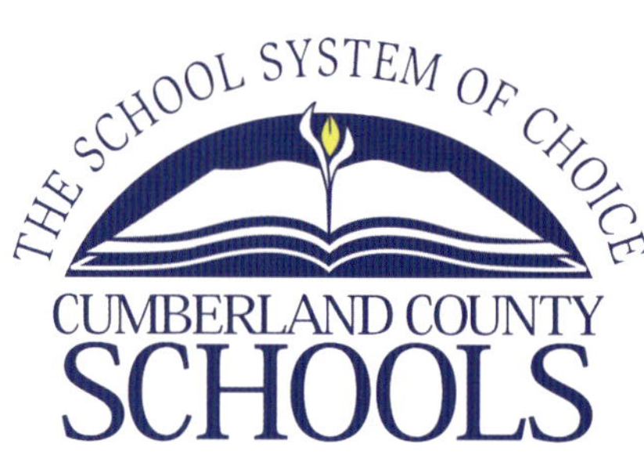

Nowhere is America's flag more respected and revered than in Fayetteville, North Carolina, home of Fort Bragg and Pope Air Force Base. Established in 1918 and named after Confederate General Braxton Bragg, the fort is currently the station of several airborne units, including the Eighty-second Airborne Division, the XVIII Airborne Corps HQ, and the United States Army Special Operations Command. This is a town filled with military personnel and their families, all dedicated to serving their country—symbolized by the red, white, and blue. Many versions of Old Glory exist throughout the country, but these flags reflect the tradition of the red stripes dominating the white in number, a tradition that was not made official until 1916. Though many U.S. flags still exist that carry a lesser number of stars, on July 4, 1960, President Dwight D. Eisenhower issued an executive order making the fifty-star flag the official flag of the United States of America. ★

Downtown Fayetteville comes alive with entertainment
during the Arts Council's monthly event known as
Fourth Friday. While galleries, shops, and bistros along
the four-block stretch of the city's downtown area open
their doors with art exhibits and retail sales, roaming
musicians like guitarist Glenn Norman Carter and
friend provide entertainment under the stars. ★

by Rod Reilly

Photo by Bruce R. Feeley

Live

What does it take to be named an "All-America City" by the National Civic League? It takes a community of people who are willing to work together to create the best possible living environment, with flourishing neighborhoods, strong economic development, unparalleled health-care facilities, highly achieving educational institutions, compelling cultural opportunities, outstanding recreational offerings, and more. Clearly, Fayetteville has all of these, as evidenced by the fact that the city has received the prestigious designation not once, but twice.

Living in Fayetteville—the county seat of Cumberland County—is an experience unlike any other. The residential options available offer something for every taste and style. For instance, the historic downtown district puts residents in the heart of the city and close to shopping, dining, and arts venues. The outlying neighborhoods of the county, on the other hand, whisk locals away to quiet dogwood-lined streets with charming homes that are perfect for families of all sizes. Then, of course, there's everything in between. And everyone, no matter where they live, has access to all of the benefits that come with a Fayetteville or Cumberland County address.

With the eighth largest hospital system in North Carolina and four full-service facilities, the area delivers world-class health care to patients with a wide variety of needs, covering everything from general medical care to surgical services, cancer care, cardiology, rehabilitation, and mental health, among many other specialties. In addition, the county's numerous public and private schools are dedicated to providing every student from kindergarten through high school with a top-quality education, thereby preparing each of them to attend such exceptional institutes of higher learning as Fayetteville State University, Methodist University, and Fayetteville Technical Community College. Once those students receive their college degrees, they will be ready to enter the workforce and the local business environment, which promises to offer them fulfilling careers—and boundless opportunities—close to home.

And when the day is done, they'll head to their single-family residences, townhouses, condos, or apartments and get ready to enjoy their downtime, just like all of the other Fayetteville and Cumberland County residents who have settled in this progressive and productive metropolitan area. With so much to see and do right around the corner or just down the street, they'll never get bored. That's the beauty of living in a bona fide All-America City. ✶

Before the Civil War, sixty-nine thousand farms, 71 percent of them under one hundred acres in size, covered North Carolina's land. For decades, scores of tenant farmers scratched out a living, earning on average a meager nine cents per day. Now, however, the state's agricultural industry competes on the world market and plays a key role in the state's economy, including that of Fayetteville and Cumberland County. On the eastern side of the city, in the community of Stedman, the Bunce Family Farm (pictured here) has been family-owned and -operated for almost a century. Equipped with state-of-the-art underground irrigation, the farm rolls on for over one thousand acres, a sea of palatable produce such as tomatoes, watermelon, and collards that are primarily shipped to consumers in the northern states.

Photo by John Chang McCurdy

FSU—PAST, PRESENT, AND FUTURE:
Uncovering Riches

It is the oldest historically black public institution of higher learning in North Carolina and currently serves over sixty-three hundred students.

There is an undiscovered treasure in Fayetteville. It isn't hidden, far from it. In fact, it has been around since 1867. Fayetteville State University often goes unnoticed, but once people visit the campus they understand what a gem it is to the community.

The history of FSU began when seven black men bought property on Gillespie Street and became a self-perpetuating board of trustees to maintain the property permanently as a site to educate black children in Fayetteville. The building that was erected was named the Howard School in honor of General O. O. Howard—head of the Freedmen's Bureau. Ten years later, the North Carolina General Assembly designated the school as a Normal School to educate black teachers. This achievement is largely attributable to the exemplary academic programs developed under the leadership of Robert Harris.

The institution acquired its present name in 1969, and in 1972 it became a constituent institution of the University of North Carolina. It is the oldest historically black public institution of higher learning in North Carolina and currently serves over sixty-three hundred students.

Today FSU is fully accredited by the Southern Association of Colleges and Schools. The university offers bachelor's degrees in forty-five areas, master's degrees in twenty-four areas, and a doctoral degree in educational leadership. The newest bachelor's programs include biotechnology, fire science, communications, forensic science, management information systems, and generic nursing.

The most recent master's programs include a master's of arts in teaching and a master's of science in criminal justice. FSU plans to increase its academic offerings and vows that every program that can receive special accreditation will do so. Several university programs already have specialized accreditation. The Collegiate Nursing Education for its generic nursing program.

The business and accounting programs are accredited by the Association to Advance Collegiate Schools of Business, the most prestigious accreditation offered, which makes the university part of an elite group of universities worldwide to have that recognition. FSU's teacher-education program has been accredited for more than fifty years by the National Council on the Accreditation of Teacher Education.

FSU is focused on providing students with the best educational atmosphere possible. The school has a number of learning communities that form small groups within the larger university. Bronco Men, for example, provides support and mentoring for male students. Statistics show that participants are more likely to graduate in four years than are males who are not in the group.

Another outstanding feature of FSU is its long standing service to the military at Fort Bragg. To serve the military community better, FSU has classrooms and faculty on base. In addition to face-to-face classes, military personnel can complete coursework online even when they are deployed to other areas.

Sports are an excellent complement to academic pursuits, and FSU has been consistently successful in athletics. Participants learn discipline, reliability, critical thinking, and tactical skills. FSU encourages involvement

(Continued on page 24)

(far left)

Students at Fayetteville State University start with the basics, such as this introductory chemistry class. From there they have a wide variety of choices. FSU offers bachelor's degrees in forty-five areas and master's degrees in twenty-four. The six most popular undergraduate majors are business administration, criminal justice, psychology, sociology, history, and elementary teacher education.

(below)

Fayetteville State University is the oldest historically black public institution of higher learning in North Carolina and currently serves over sixty-three hundred students. Many things have changed over the years, but the joy upon graduation is eternal. Students here are celebrating at the school's 140th spring commencement.

Photo by Diane Kirkland

Photo by Bruce R. Feeley

(left)

The Fayetteville community frequently enjoys campus programs such as the FSU Concert Choir and String Ensemble performing Handel's Messiah under the direction of Marvin Curtis. Other programs, like the Distinguished Speaker Series, are also free and open to the public.

(below)

Fayetteville State University, the oldest historically black public institution of higher learning in North Carolina, is a member of the Central Intercollegiate Athletic Association. Students take pride in their marching band and the fact that in recent years, the Bronco teams have brought home twenty-two championships in football, basketball, golf, volleyball, tennis, bowling, and softball.

(Fayetteville State University continued from page 23)

in both intramural and competitive programs, but emphasizes to students the importance of staying grounded and earning their degrees.

Fayetteville residents often enjoy special events on campus such as the Chancellor's Distinguished Speakers' Series and the Performing and Fine Arts Series. In addition they rely on WFSS to provide them with NPR programming as well as locally produced jazz and classical music shows.

As part of another farsighted FSU program, elementary, middle, and high school students are taking a ten-session course focusing on Chinese language and culture. FSU provides a strong Asian language program so that students can be better prepared to flourish in the global economy of the future.

FSU has made its own impact on the Fayetteville community's economy. A

Photo by Bruce R. Feeley

recent study showed the university generates $2.93 in economic activity for every $1 appropriated.

There are a number of ways to explore FSU, but all facets of this outstanding institution clearly indicate it is indeed a jewel. ★

Photo by Erin Brethauer

Photo by John Chang McCurdy

(above)

Each spring since 1992, students at FSU have looked forward to the Miss Fayetteville State University Scholarship Pageant. Contestants must have a high scholastic average and compete in several categories, including interview, sportswear, talent, and evening gown. The popular event is free and open to the public. The winner in 2007 was Lisa Harris, who became the official hostess for the university. Her court included Tyinna Johnson and Amber Bernard.

(left)

Part of the mission of Fayetteville State University is to offer a sound liberal arts foundation, which includes providing students with the opportunity to explore and develop new talents. Visual arts majors get hands-on experience dealing with various media, such as working with watercolors.

On this beautiful fall afternoon, a good portion of Methodist University's approximately twenty-three hundred students—who come from forty-four states and thirty-one countries—spent the day enjoying homecoming activities. MU is an NCAA Division III school that offers nineteen varsity sports for men and women. The Monarchs regularly compete for conference, regional, and national championships. ✦

Communities Coming Together

Photo by Bruce R. Feeley

Preschool children and their teachers enjoy Community Relations Day, a morning of free activities and shows sponsored by the Partnership for Children of Cumberland County. The annual event is for child-care facilities that work with PFC's Child Care Solutions Department. ✶

Spending time outdoors in Fayetteville gives one a real sense of our community's hometown quality, and making sure our city and its parks stay green and shady is the responsibility of our Parks Division and personnel like Dewayne McLain (left) and James Smith. Whether you visit one of our regional parks or a smaller neighborhood park, you and your family will be immersed in a comforting, lush, green landscape.

CITY OF FAYETTEVILLE:
Making a Better Place for All

Fayetteville is a gathering place for young and old, married and single, soldiers and civilians.

Birds chirp in the shade trees lining the brick sidewalks of a downtown main street. The careful restoration of historic buildings housing shops and apartment lofts is evident. Stop for coffee and hear music wafting on the breezes, fountains whose tumbling water soothes, the chatter of families or friends meeting. Fayetteville is a gathering place for young and old, married and single, soldiers and civilians. It is a diverse community made richer by the commingling of old and new, its parks and neighborhoods, bustling streets and entertainment opportunities.

A neighbor to Fort Bragg and Pope Air Force Base, home to a regional airport, and with access to Interstate 95, Fayetteville holds a strategic position in the southeastern part of North Carolina. It is a place of history and culture, affordable housing and education, beauty and opportunity, all contributing to a well-deserved award as an All-America City.

Ensuring that it remains a place some 174,000 residents want to call home are the professionals in city government, individuals who work hard to fulfill their mission of "Making Fayetteville a Better Place for All."

Some of the ways they work toward that goal are through the Community Development Department, which provides opportunities to all citizens in need of decent, safe, and affordable housing. This department also creates positive economic development situations in assisting

businesses that provide jobs for people with low to moderate income and in the expansion of the tax base.

Clean streets, convenient sidewalks, and adequate water drainage are also the city's responsibility. Through its engineering and infrastructure services, the city provides for the design, construction, and maintenance of these vital components as well as for the traffic signs, signals, and markings that keep drivers and pedestrians safe. The city also manages its stormwater runoff in order to ensure quality is maintained in the area's lakes and streams.

Maintaining the natural beauty of many parks and recreation facilities falls under the city's auspices, as does sanitation coordination—including recycling, waste collection, and waste management.

The city keeps its residents safe through the provision of police and fire services, and it promotes equal opportunity through its Human Relations Commission, an eleven-member board of city and county representatives who advise the governing body on ways to advance harmony among racial and ethnic groups.

Fayetteville is governed by an elected city council, composed of a mayor and members representing five local districts whose citizens are encouraged to provide input. As a whole, the council's activities center on continual improvement through greater business diversity, more efficient city government, community unity, city beautification, the revitalization of downtown, and just making Fayetteville an increasingly greater place to live. ★

Traffic signal management engineer Carl McCartney monitors main thoroughfares through the City of Fayetteville's state-of-the-art traffic signal system, which tracks traffic flow and signal issues daily to ensure that Fayetteville's roads are safe and traffic is as free-flowing as possible. Because roadways are such a vital part of our transportation system, the Traffic Engineering Division is charged with keeping our traffic signals, street signs, and street markings in working order.

All Photos by Greg Foster

Since its founding in 1796, Evans Metropolitan African Methodist Episcopal Zion Church has been a place where people have come together for Christian worship and camaraderie. In addition to an inspiring Sunday service, the church offers its members a number of activities that encourage involvement, including bible study, choir, clubs and committees, recognition programs, an annual golf classic, and more. The church, established by black freedom preacher Henry Evans, whose body was entombed beneath the structure following his death, remains one of the world's oldest African Methodist Episcopal Zion churches and was listed as a National Historic Site in 1983. ✱

LWSHOMES.COM:
Where You'll Find the Right Price, the Right Place, the Right Home

"If a buyer is looking for specific amenities, they can go on the Web site and look for those things."

When looking for a new home in Cumberland and western Harnett counties, the best place to start is LWSHOMES.com. "It's a one-stop shop for looking at houses," says Larry Wayne Strother, owner and Web site namesake. "The site is a single source where any potential buyer, or any real estate agent, can go to get all the information they need."

More than just a listing of Strother developments, the site is actually a collection of multiple neighborhoods that are under development by a wide range of builders. The idea of displaying the listings in one location, says Strother, was to relieve builders from the demands of marketing and selling their properties and allow them to focus on the thing they do best. "They're builders of homes, and this allows them to spend their time building houses," says Strother. "They're not focused on getting exposure for themselves. They'd rather let us deal with all the factors that get those structures sold."

At any given time, a dozen or more neighborhoods are listed on the site, easily mapped out to show their relationship to places such as the city of Fayetteville and the Fort Bragg military installation. Choose a neighborhood, and a list of available properties with basic information is displayed. Another click reveals photos, additional details, price, and a wide selection of available floor plans.

Looking for a home with just the right amount of space, a fireplace, and a living room with a view? That's the beauty of LWSHOMES.com. Through the Dream Home Finder, or other similar areas of the site, selecting a floor plan will lead to the home's location in multiple neighborhoods with just the click of a mouse. "If a buyer is looking for specific amenities, they can go on the Web site and look for those things," says Strother. "And with our wide variety of subdivisions, if one location doesn't fit your needs, then another one possibly will." For even more choices, Strother's separate real estate entities can connect buyers to a wealth of existing home options.

Buyers using the LWSHOMES.com site can also view their home as it is being built, with photos of the construction process uploaded on a regular basis.

In addition, each neighborhood is staffed by a knowledgeable LWSHOMES.com representative, available to answers questions on any property. Providing such a service is something that Strother takes very personally.

"All we have to offer people is service," says the local real estate industry veteran. "And we recognize the importance of making people want to do business with us. Plus, LWSHOMES.com is me. I'm putting my name on the line, and as a result, I want everyone out there benefiting from the very best service we can provide." ✩

(far left)

Marketing representatives based in each neighborhood listed on LWSHOMES.com are trained and certified to offer on-site assistance to customers and clients.

(left)

Larry W. Strother, president of LWS Homes, is a thirty-year veteran of the real estate industry. Strother and his team have the insight and inventory to help anyone realize the dream of homeownership.

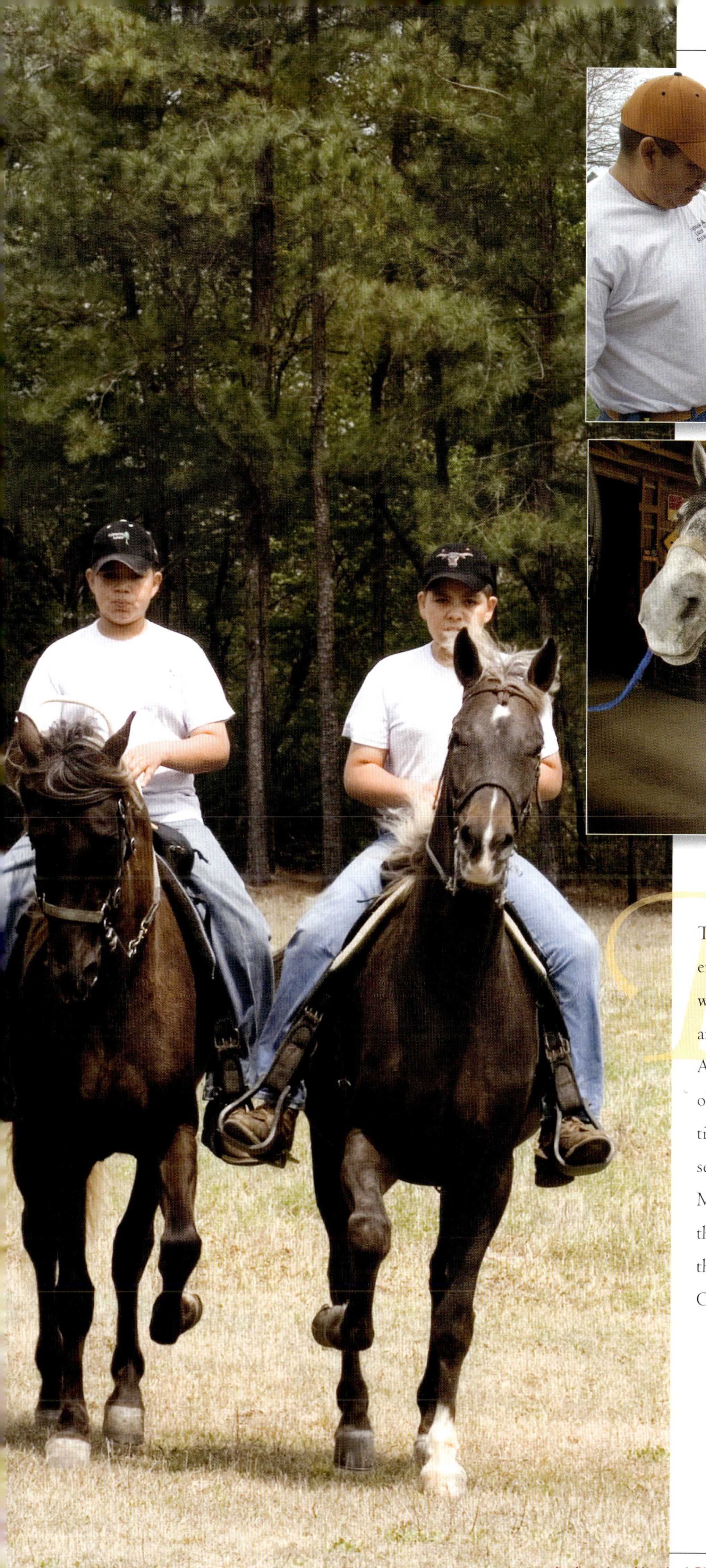

All Photos by Bruce R. Feeley

The heart of the Cypress Lakes Community in southern Cumberland County is Cypress Lakes Stables, where champion horses are bred and trained. Owned and operated by the family of the late Alfred "Big Al" Prewitt, the farm was developed on acreage of the old Rainey Family Farm when Big Al, a Kentucky native, settled in Fayetteville after serving in the Eighty-second Airborne Division at Fort Bragg and married Merle Rainey, daughter of the personal physician of the Rockefellers. The original forty acres has grown to thousands to make up the thriving Cypress Lakes Community, with homes and a golf course. ✶

All Photos by John Chang McCurdy

FAYETTEVILLE AREA CONVENTION AND VISITORS BUREAU:
Promoting America's Hometown

No matter the need, the FACVB serves as a vital source of information and planning assistance.

Fayetteville and Cumberland County are becoming popular travel destinations, thanks in part to the promotional efforts of the Fayetteville Area Convention and Visitors Bureau.

A private, nonprofit corporation acting under contract with the Tourism Development Authority, the FACVB shapes the vision, develops the strategy, and implements the most effective programs to position Cumberland County as a destination for conventions and individual travel.

No matter the need, whether reunions, religious conferences, sports events, historical tours, or business conventions, the FACVB serves as a vital source of information and planning assistance. And the bureau continues to offer innovative resources, including a customizable tour planner, CustomizeIT! available on www.VisitFayettevilleNC.com.

Each of the bureau's four departments—sales, communications, visitor services, and administration—closely monitors the trends and issues that affect the industry and responds accordingly. Working through organizations such as the Reunion Network, the Society of Government Meeting Professionals, and Religious Conference Management Association, the staff stays up to date on the needs of planners and secures business leads for the community.

The bureau offers personalized and friendly service you would expect in America's Hometown. "Our approach is not 'cookie cutter,' explains FACVB president and CEO John Meroski. "We customize our services depending on the needs of the individual or group." Whether it's providing customized proposals from hotels, conducting site visits, staffing welcome tables, or planning off-site tours, the bureau extends a hometown feeling to all.

The bureau also acts as keeper of the Cumberland County brand. The Fayetteville & Cumberland County Brand Standards Guide was introduced in December 2006. "It's so important for a community to market itself cohesively, to ensure we all have a similar look and feel," says Meroski. In addition to graphic representation of the Cumberland County brand, the Brand Standards Guide highlights the importance of branding and how the county's brand developed.

Aside from convincing people to visit, the bureau also services those who are already visiting. Guests are welcome to drop by the bureau's main office at 245 Person Street or its satellite visitor centers at the Fayetteville Transportation Museum or Cross Creek Mall. Each location provides a wealth of information, all with friendly service.

For its service to Cumberland County, the FACVB is a regular recipient of numerous industry awards and recognitions. In 2006 alone, the bureau received three Destination Marketing Achievement Awards from the North Carolina Association of Convention & Visitor Bureaus and the Southeast Tourism Society's Top 20 events award for Fayetteville's Dogwood and International Folk festivals.

Perhaps the greatest reward is the bureau's positive impact on the region's economy. Currently, Cumberland County is tenth among North Carolina's one hundred counties in economic impact from travel and tourism. Additionally, travel spending keeps forty-one hundred residents employed; generates over $25 million a year in lodging, sales, and state taxes; and brings in over $316 million overall. That's good news for those who make Cumberland County their home. ★

(far left)
Fayetteville Area CVB positions Cumberland County as a destination for conventions, sporting events, and individual travel. Each week, more than fifteen hundred visitor guides are distributed to guests and newcomers to the Fayetteville area. The bureau's hard work shows: according to a recent survey, 72 percent of visitors would recommend the Fayetteville area to their friends.

(below)
Director of sales Myron Jones (left) talks to prospective meeting planners about bringing their event to greater Fayetteville. With everything from charming bed-and-breakfasts to nationally recognized hotel chains to a full-service hotel and conference center, Fayetteville easily accommodates any meeting's size and budget.

Visitors have to come early and stay late in order to take advantage of the thirty different events during the weekend of the Fayetteville Dogwood Festival, which is held each April. Founded in 1982, the festival now includes national and local musicians, artists, arts and crafts vendors, food stands, sporting events, street dances, carnival rides, children's activities—in other words, something for everyone. Its original purpose was to promote Fayetteville, and judging from the increasing crowds, it has certainly done that. ★

NANTUCKET

COLORADO
ROCKY MOUNTAINS

FUN SLIDE
POPCORN
COTTON CANDY ★ CANDY APPLES
COUNTRY LEMONADE
DRINKS
HOT DOG

All Photos by Bruce R. Feeley

Jeff Mozingo (left), vice president, and Jim Mozingo, president, are dedicated to insuring their clients' assets, safety, and well-being at Independent Insurance Group.

INDEPENDENT INSURANCE GROUP, INC.:
Quality Coverage, Optimal Service

"You want to feel comfortable with the level of coverage you have and to trust your agent to provide the service you deserve."

Keeping up with regulations in the insurance industry and trying to decide which companies can best serve your needs can be quite a challenge. Independent Agents/Trusted Choice Agents such as Independent Insurance Group, Inc. (IIG) represent several insurance companies. By aligning with reputable carriers, they can offer a wide choice of insurance products to help protect your home, your family, and your business.

Founded in 1992 by Jim Mozingo, IIG is a licensed property and casualty insurance agency in North Carolina, South Carolina, Georgia, and Virginia. Under his leadership, IIG has grown to a multimillion-dollar agency in the property and casualty and the life and health fields.

"You want to feel comfortable with the level of coverage you have and to trust your agent to provide the service you deserve," Mozingo said. "That is what our customers have come to appreciate."

IIG's well-trained agents sell and service individual home and auto policies (including renters, vacation home, umbrella liability, rental property, recreational vehicle, boat, and valuable property coverage). Businesses can trust IIG for their commercial insurance needs as well, including general and professional liability, workers' compensation, property, and auto coverage.

The Independent Insurance Agents of North Carolina (IIANC), a statewide association representing more than one thousand independent insurance agencies in North Carolina, provides industry knowledge and superb commitment to its agents. Mozingo has served in many capacities on the IIANC board, including his current position of District 6 representative. The agents and staff of IIG are committed to serving you as well. ✳

Chris Harrison (left), president of EbenConcepts, and Jim Mozingo, president of IIG Inc., united their employee benefits divisions to offer exclusive employee benefits products and supreme service to employers of all sizes.

EBENCONCEPTS:
Enhancing Employee Benefit Offerings

Employers are constantly faced with tough decisions when deciding how to offer the most comprehensive health benefits without exceeding the budget. They want to trust the people they choose to provide health care to their employees. After all, employees are a company's greatest asset.

EbenConcepts, led by president Chris Harrison, is a brokerage company with more than twenty offices nationwide and headquartered in Fayetteville, North Carolina. The company's goal is to provide employers and employees with unique insurance products and services coupled with exclusive solutions to simplify the benefits administration process.

How does EbenConcepts make life simple for its clients? For starters, the consolidated billing feature means employers receive just one bill with their benefits carriers' monthly totals on it. Employers love writing one check for all benefits, freeing their time to focus on more productive issues.

They also provide affordable Section 125 administration with flex accounts and debit cards, comprehensive human resource services, and complete COBRA administration to ensure compliance with strict federal regulations.

Finally, their exclusive arrangements with certain life and dental carriers include no participation requirements, renewal rate caps, and $150,000 guaranteed-issue voluntary life and AD&D.

For unparalleled customer service and the extra touches that relieve much of the stress from HR professionals and small business owners, EbenConcepts is the exclusive choice in the health benefits arena. Along with its sister company, IIG Inc. (led by Jim Mozingo, vice president of EbenConcepts), they help companies find effective solutions for every type of insurance need. ✶

EbenConcepts is a brokerage company with more than twenty offices nationwide and headquartered in Fayetteville, North Carolina.

Photo by Rod Reilly

Thousands of people mark their calendars for Fayetteville's regular Fourth Friday event, and then they show up! They don't dare miss the free refreshments, music, and mixed festivities occurring along the full four blocks of the city's safe and eclectic historic district. As they join in a massive gallery crawl, they also browse the boutiques and bistros, sample some cheese and wine, or pause for an impromptu show by a street magician. This Fourth Friday soiree featured the Arts Education of the Cumberland County Schools System, showcasing the visual arts of high school students in the categories of drawing, painting, and sculpture. Meanwhile, the American Indian Dance Troupe, the E. E. Smith Performance Troup, the Douglas Byrd Band, and the Jack Britt High School's Legato proved that the performing arts are also talents on display.

Building the Workforce of the Future

Cumberland County, like the state of North Carolina, is on the brink of an exciting future. As the state continues to transition from a manufacturing to an information-based economy, Cumberland County mirrors that evolution. It is building on a strong service economy and recruiting high-tech, information-based businesses that will provide the best-paying jobs in the future. To do this, the county is developing innovative programs to provide workers the skills and training they need to compete for the jobs of the twenty-first century.

The Cumberland County Workforce Development Board and professional staff of the Workforce Development Center administer Workforce Investment Act funds to support building the academic and occupational skills of the county's youth, adults, dislocated workers, and senior citizens. The Workforce Development Center is a partner agency of the North Carolina Joblink Career Center system. This partnership offers residents a variety of excellent employment and training opportunities designed to meet the challenges of an increasingly competitive global economy.

Zocanise Flores (right) talks with the assistant director of the child care facility at Fayetteville Technical Community College, Heather McKeithan. Zocanise is a recent graduate of FTCC and another success story for Workforce Development in Cumberland County. The spouse of a soldier assigned to Fort Bragg and deployed overseas, Zocanise was a beneficiary of the Military Spouses Transition Services Project, enabling her to pursue a double degree. She has earned an associate's degree in early childhood education and early childhood administration, maintaining a 4.0 GPA throughout her studies. She graduated magna cum laude in May 2007. The various programs administered by Workforce Development in Cumberland County have prepared many people for meaningful careers in the twenty-first century.

The agency plays a local role in the state's Business Services initiative to assist business and industry in optimizing connections to services offered by the Workforce Development Board and the Joblink Career Center. The professionals involved in this important work share a common goal of developing and sustaining a globally competitive workforce that will positively affect the economic well-being and quality of life for Cumberland County residents. The Cumberland County Workforce Development Center was one of six programs in the state assisting Hurricane Katrina evacuees with job searches and placement as well as case management.

Cumberland County's Workforce Development professionals are proud of a successful program designed to help displaced workers who have lost jobs as a consequence of a military transfer. So many spouses lose lucrative jobs when they follow their soldier or airman to a new post. But spouses at Fort Bragg and Pope Air Force Base have been provided the opportunity to attend local colleges, at no cost to them, to receive training in a new skill. Qualifying applicants even receive their books at no cost. Spouses enrolled in this program have strengthened the local workforce even as they strengthen their future employability wherever life and military service may take them. ✭

Sarah Wilson is learning the finer points of automobile mechanics at Fayetteville Technical Community College. She is a participant in Cumberland County's Workforce Development Dislocated Worker program, having lost a manufacturing job when the plant where she worked closed. The dislocated worker program assists Sarah with her tuition, books, and supplies as she pursues an associate's degree in the automotive systems technology curriculum. Sarah says it was challenging to return to school, twenty years after graduating from high school, but she maintains a very high GPA and expects to obtain her degree in May 2008. She looks forward to being known as Sarah Wilson, mechanic.

CUMBERLAND COUNTY, NORTH CAROLINA:
Celebrating Our Past, Embracing Our Future

Cumberland County is a large county, embracing more than six hundred square miles of diverse land, ranging from fertile farmland to sandy soil to red clay.

Cumberland County, North Carolina, in the early twenty-first century is evolving into a multi-dimensional community, populated by more than three hundred thousand people of diverse races, ethnicities, creeds, interests, and talents. Their future is a bright one, as the county achieves success in developing an economy that includes, but is not limited to, a thriving retail sector, agricultural endeavors, high-tech industry, and the presence of America's most populated military base, Fort Bragg.

As one of one hundred counties in North Carolina, Cumberland County is responsible for certain governmental services to its population, including funding the local school system, providing law enforcement, ensuring public health, preparing for emergencies, and disposing of solid waste, among many other services that enhance the quality of life. The county functions with a board of commissioners comprising seven elected leaders who work

closely with a county manager and professional staff in administering various laws, statutes, and policies, and providing the services to which citizens are entitled.

Centered in the southeastern North Carolina region, Cumberland County is a large county, embracing more than six hundred square miles of diverse land, ranging from fertile farmland to sandy soil to red clay. A large section, more than 161,000 acres, is taken up by Fort Bragg, with drop zones, firing ranges, and training fields as well as

(continued on page 48)

The Cumberland County Sheriff's Office is an effective law enforcement agency, with deputies trained in a variety of crime-fighting skills. It is one of only three sheriff's offices in North Carolina accredited by the Commission on Accreditation for Law Enforcement Agencies.

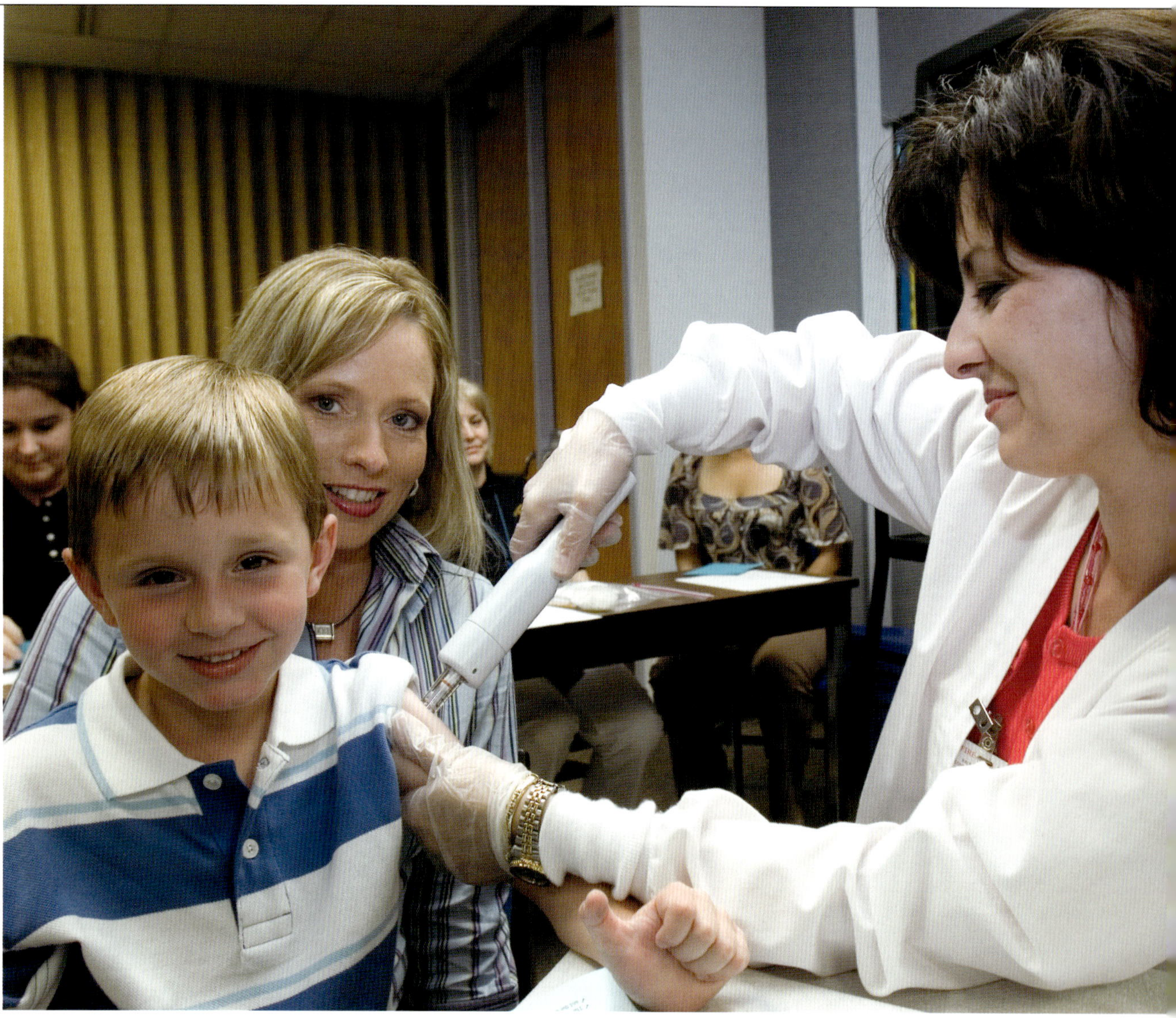

(right)

Cumberland County's Department of Public Health is involved in many aspects of the community, from restaurant inspections to the health of schoolchildren. Here, a young student receives an immunization, smiling all the while.

(below)

Cumberland County Board of Elections employee Joyce Carter (left) points out to her colleague Angie Amaro various features of the voting machines used by voters in Cumberland County. There are more than 175,000 registered voters in Cumberland County.

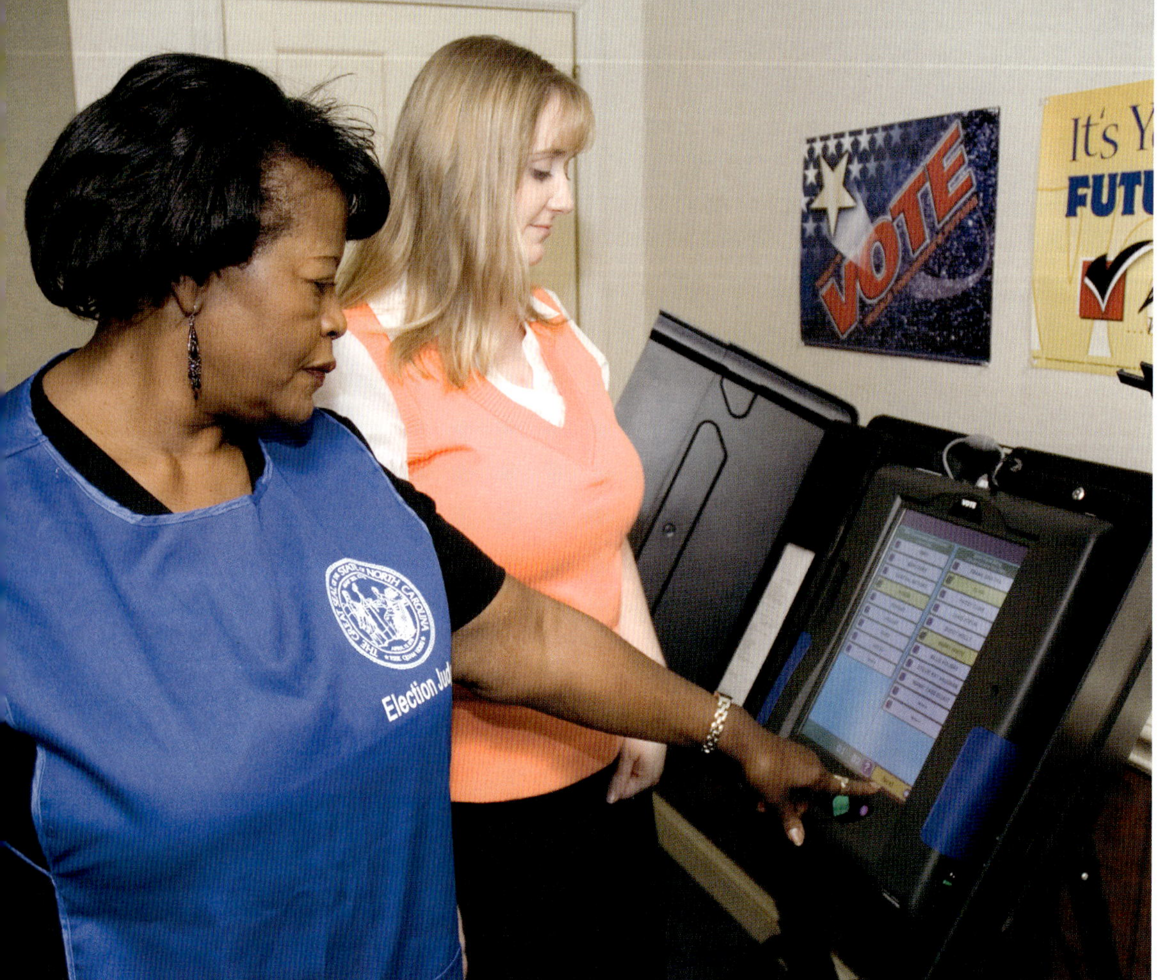

Photo by Diane Kirkland

Photo by Alan S. Weiner

(County of Cumberland continued from page 47)

residential areas with shopping centers, social clubs, golf courses, and a library for soldiers and their families.

Pine tree forests are abundant, hardwood trees thrive, and the state flower, the dogwood, blooms in rampant profusion in early spring. Streams, lakes, creeks, and ponds are found throughout the county, which is bisected by the Cape Fear River. One of Cumberland County's most fascinating natural resources, the river is what first drew settlers to the area more than 250 years ago.

Cumberland County is home to nine municipalities, Fayetteville being the largest with more than 175,000 citizens. The smaller municipalities, each with its own distinct character and charm, are Spring Lake, Hope Mills, Stedman, Linden, Godwin, Wade, and Falcon.

Two and a half centuries of growth and change have brought Cumberland County into a new era. In 2005, the Base Realignment and Closure Commission decided that the headquarters of the U.S. Army's Forces Command, at Fort McPherson, Georgia, should move to Fort Bragg, as should Fort McPherson's headquarters of the army's Reserve Command. The influx of these soldiers, civilian employees, and family

(Continued on page 50)

Cumberland County's Historic Court House is a stately downtown Fayetteville presence and still houses some offices of county government. The courtroom seen here, however, no longer functions as a courtroom. It has been beautifully restored to be as it was in 1925 when the building opened. The court house has been replaced by a more modern building, opened in 1978.

Photo by Alan S. Weiner

(County of Cumberland continued from page 49)

members into the Fort Bragg community, to occur about 2010, will boost the county's population significantly. More importantly, it is expected to attract high-tech, defense-related businesses to the area eager to provide Fort Bragg, a huge consumer of many different materials, services, and products, what it needs.

Cumberland County is indeed a great place to be—whether raising a family, transacting business, or simply living a satisfying life to the fullest! ★

Cumberland County's Animal Control Center occupies a new, state-of-the-art facility in the county's Industrial Park. Here, animal control officers Melissa Hook and Candace McRay (background) give two of their charges a good bit of exercise.

She might be a tad past prime NFL age, but this young lady still has a shot at the big time. By participating in the Annual Mid-Carolina Senior Games, she can qualify for the state finals, and from there, the National Senior Olympics. The theme of the regional Mid-Carolina Senior Games is "Reach Out to New Horizons," and reach out, they do. The football throw is just one of many events that more than four hundred older adults from Cumberland, Sampson, and Harnett counties can participate in each year. They bowl, they swim, they golf, they play tennis, bocce, basketball, and shuffleboard. They even compete in spin casting, showing off their aim gained from years of fishing. Organizers think promoting health is also all about the mind and spirit, so the games feature the Silver Arts Program, where older adults who perhaps aren't as athletic can participate creatively in the visual, literary, performing, and heritage arts (woodworking and quilting, for example). You go, girl! ★

STATES ARMY
RNE UNITS
STATES ARMY
AL OPERATIONS U
L OF HONOR

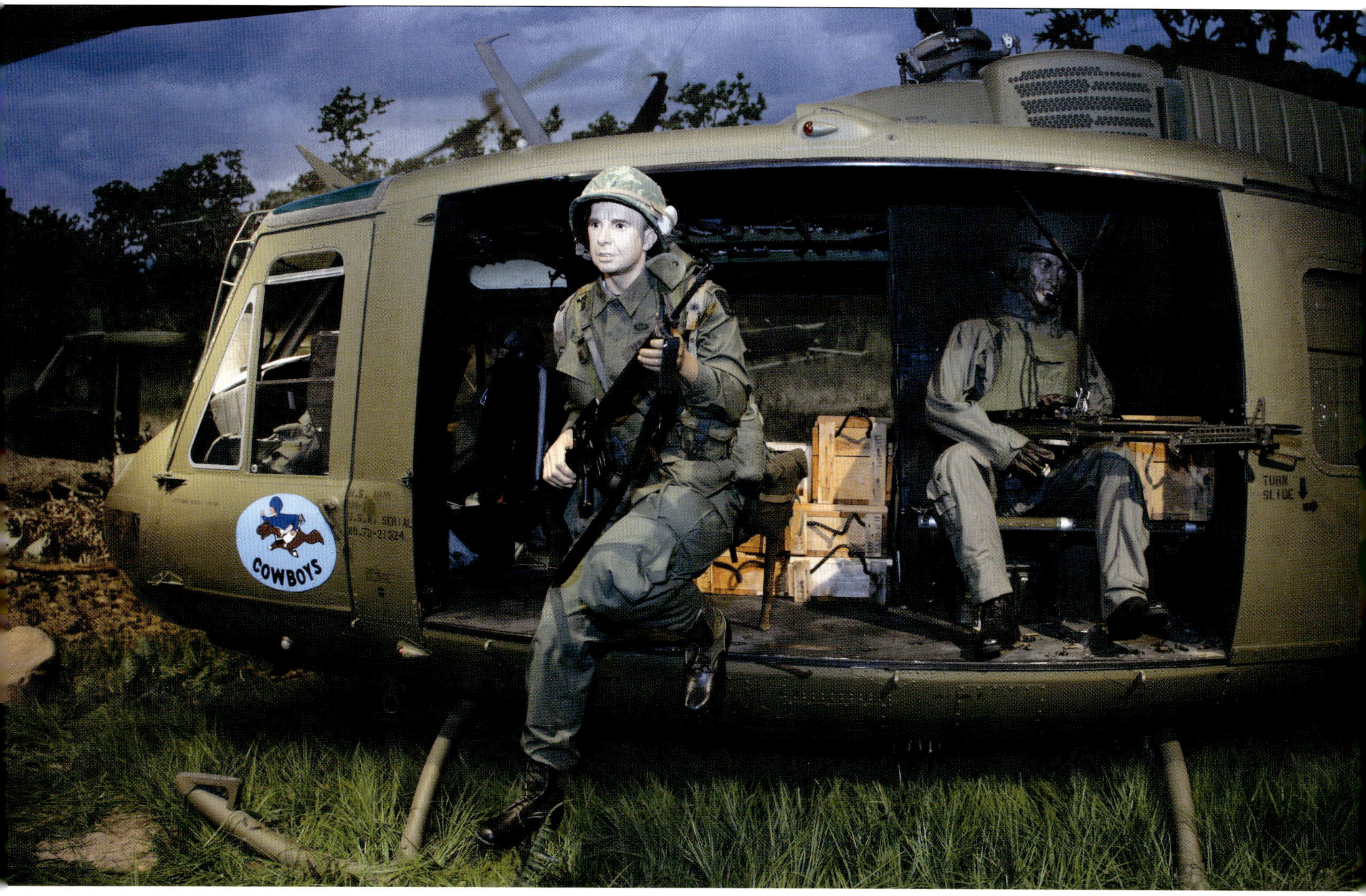

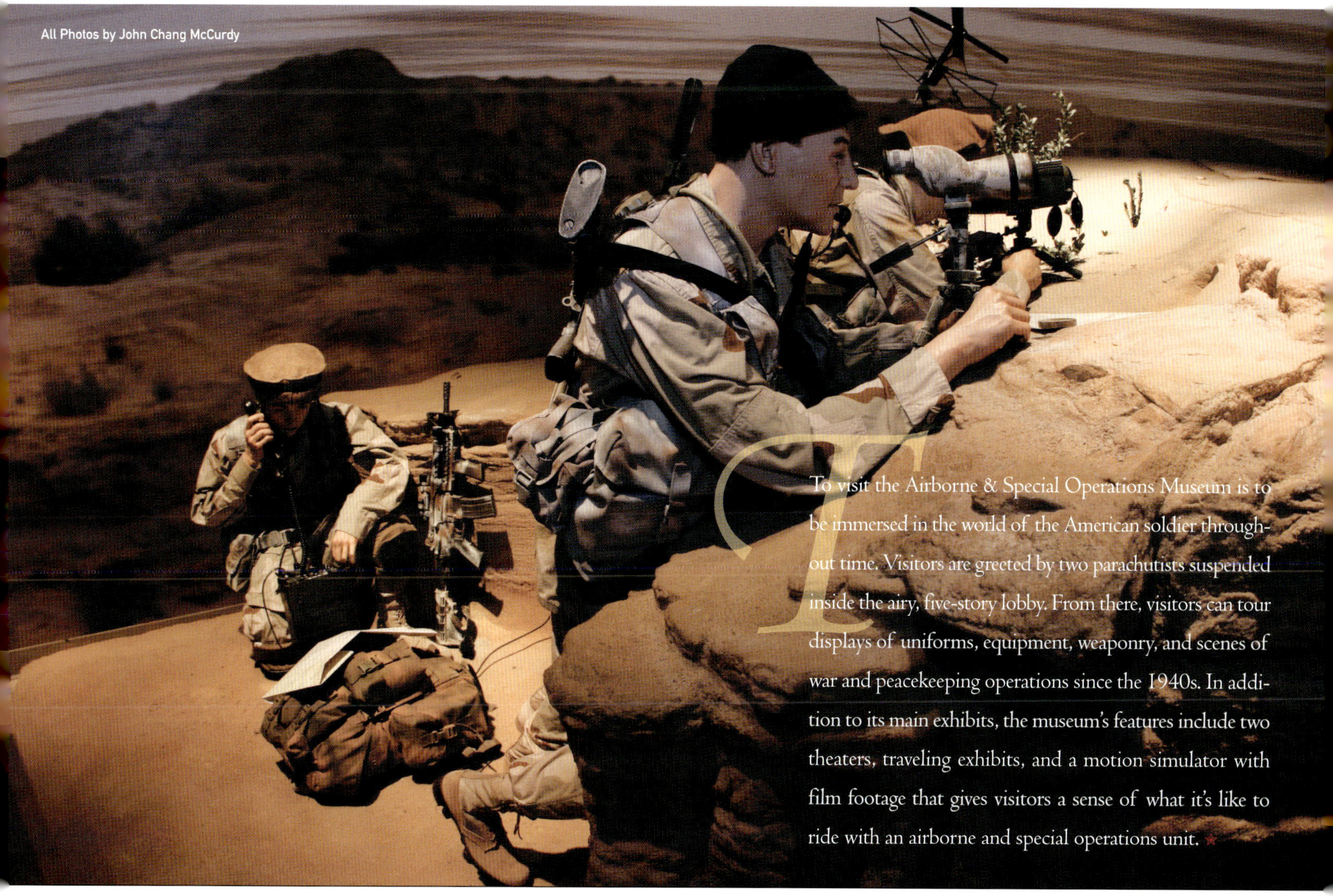

All Photos by John Chang McCurdy

To visit the Airborne & Special Operations Museum is to be immersed in the world of the American soldier throughout time. Visitors are greeted by two parachutists suspended inside the airy, five-story lobby. From there, visitors can tour displays of uniforms, equipment, weaponry, and scenes of war and peacekeeping operations since the 1940s. In addition to its main exhibits, the museum's features include two theaters, traveling exhibits, and a motion simulator with film footage that gives visitors a sense of what it's like to ride with an airborne and special operations unit.

Golfers in the Fayetteville area won't have any trouble finding the right course, but they may have trouble narrowing down the choices. With twenty courses, 360 holes, and nineteen miles of fairways, Fayetteville is a golfer's dream. Raymond Floyd and Chip Beck cut their teeth out on Fayetteville's fairways, and Davis Love III and Willard Byrd have both designed courses in the area. An added bonus: thanks to Fayetteville's temperate climate, you can enjoy the sport year-round. For complete information on golf throughout the region, contact the Fayetteville Area Convention & Visitors Bureau.

Potential has no boundaries, and neither should the classroom. Here, an elementary science class is taught in the outdoor "exploratorium." Making science come alive means moving from the textbook to activities that engage the student. Activities may include creating a nature trail, bird watching, museum visits, field trips, conservation awareness, and a variety of on-campus projects that get students actively involved in the scientific process and the lessons that nature presents. When you visit classrooms in the Cumberland County Schools, you may find students holding an exact replica of a human bone and discussing where it is located in their bodies, or tracking weather in a foreign country where a deployed parent is stationed—all interesting, engaging, and personal. ✭

Methodist University was established as a joint venture of the citizens of Fayetteville/Cumberland County and the North Carolina Conference of the United Methodist Church. It is the city's only independent four-year university. Smaller classes allow Professor Peggy Hinson to give lots of attention to art majors (left to right) Christina Erben, Larissa Wilson, and Michael Hamilton as they work on projects for her ceramic sculpture class.

METHODIST UNIVERSITY:
Engage, Enrich, Empower

Few words better portray the Methodist University experience than those in the headline above. A Methodist University education starts with engagement. With just twenty-two hundred students, more than seventy organizations, and a twelve-to-one student/faculty ratio, MU students are involved. They are known, they are heard, and they make things happen. They are engaged.

Once engaged, MU students go on to become part of an environment that enriches their minds and their lives— spiritually and academically. The chance to participate in intercollegiate athletics, community service, extracurricular activities, and one-on-one exchanges with professors provides MU students with the opportunity to gather knowledge, embody it, grow from it, and put it to use in the world. They are enriched.

With just twenty-two hundred students, more than seventy organizations, and a twelve-to-one student/faculty ratio, MU students are involved.

By graduation, having had so many opportunities to try, to succeed, to fail, to manage, to ask questions, and to search for answers, students leave MU knowing their subject, knowing themselves, and having the confidence to strike out in the world. They are empowered.

The experience does not end with graduation. Methodist University's support continues as alumni build their lives and their dreams. Alumni are engaged through the alumni magazine, the university's Web site, homecoming weekends, and gatherings in cities throughout the United States. They are enriched by programs, learning opportunities, and offerings geared to meet their needs. They are empowered with an impressive network that enables them to connect to the MU alumni community. Methodist University is a vibrant resource for a generation and a community on the move. ✦

Historic downtown Fayetteville is a fitting location for St. John's Episcopal Church for many reasons. Founded in 1817, the house of worship is recognized as the city's first Episcopal church and today boasts more than seven hundred communicants. It has had eighteen rectors in its long history. The building itself, which is listed on the National Register of Historic Places, features several significant hallmarks, including a small single manual pipe organ, a Victorian Baptism Font, and the exquisite chancel. In addition, the altar is outlined by five magnificent Resurrection Windows, which comprise the last set of stained-glass windows made by Mayer and Company of New York and Munich. An additional window in the rear of the church is just as beautiful and includes a signature fleur-de-lis design that represents the Holy Trinity and the Blessed Virgin Mary. Together, the windows were first displayed at the World's Fair in California in 1890. Today, they welcome parishioners every week for the Holy Eucharist and stand as a testament to the enduring faith held dear by many of Fayetteville's residents. ✶

CONDO*Concepts:*
Builds Lifestyles
Everywhere You Want to Be

Owning a home is not only one of the smartest investments we can make; it is also one of the most satisfying. In choosing our home, we define not only where, but also how we want to live.

CONDO*Concepts* was developed with just this idea in mind. Owners Tommy Bradford and Ralph Huff have earned a reputation for excellence in real estate development and new home construction throughout Fayetteville and the surrounding region. Committed to innovative, quality design and construction, they don't just build homes, they build lifestyles.

As the luxury condominium specialists in the region, Bradford and Huff understand how to meet their buyers' growing desire for hassle-free home ownership. CONDO*Concepts* is selling several impressive new condominium communities that offer all the advantages of home ownership with none of the hassles. Although unique in their design and location, each community features quality craftsmanship, the most sought-after upscale features and finest amenities, and a no-maintenance environment that leaves residents free to enjoy their time—free to enjoy their lives.

Each community is designed to accommodate a variety of interests and needs. 216 Fountainhead, for instance, offers all the advantages of living in the heart of historic downtown Fayetteville, with easy access to the area's restaurants, shops, and galleries. Landfall and Woodland Villas are located minutes outside the city's core, but still remain convenient to favorite dining and shopping facilities, Fort Bragg, and Pope AFB. Just northeast, McArthur Landing offers active residents a vacationlike-

Committed to innovative, quality design and construction, they don't just build homes, they build lifestyle.

atmosphere without leaving home. A beautiful residence club with spa-like fountains, fully equipped fitness center, pool, and putting green are just a few of its enticing amenities. Serene country-club living is offered even further north, at the elegant Fairway Pointe at Anderson Creek Club.

Buyers who choose a CONDO*Concepts* home can rest assured that their relationship doesn't end with the sale. The company's team of highly trained customer care representatives keeps buyers informed throughout every step of the process. The CONDO*Concepts* sales team also works closely with construction management, lending institutions, appraisers, and closing agents to ensure that each buyer's unique needs are met.

Upon completion of their new home, buyers receive a thorough orientation and predelivery inspection. During this time, representatives also make sure that buyers are well acquainted with their homeowner's warranty, as well as the community's individual amenities and its homeowner association.

CONDO*Concepts* is committed to crafting thoughtfully planned communities designed for every lifestyle. Their approach offers buyers throughout Fayetteville and the surrounding areas the opportunity to enjoy the luxury feel of custom construction, the casual feel of a carefree lifestyle, and the just-right feel of home. ★

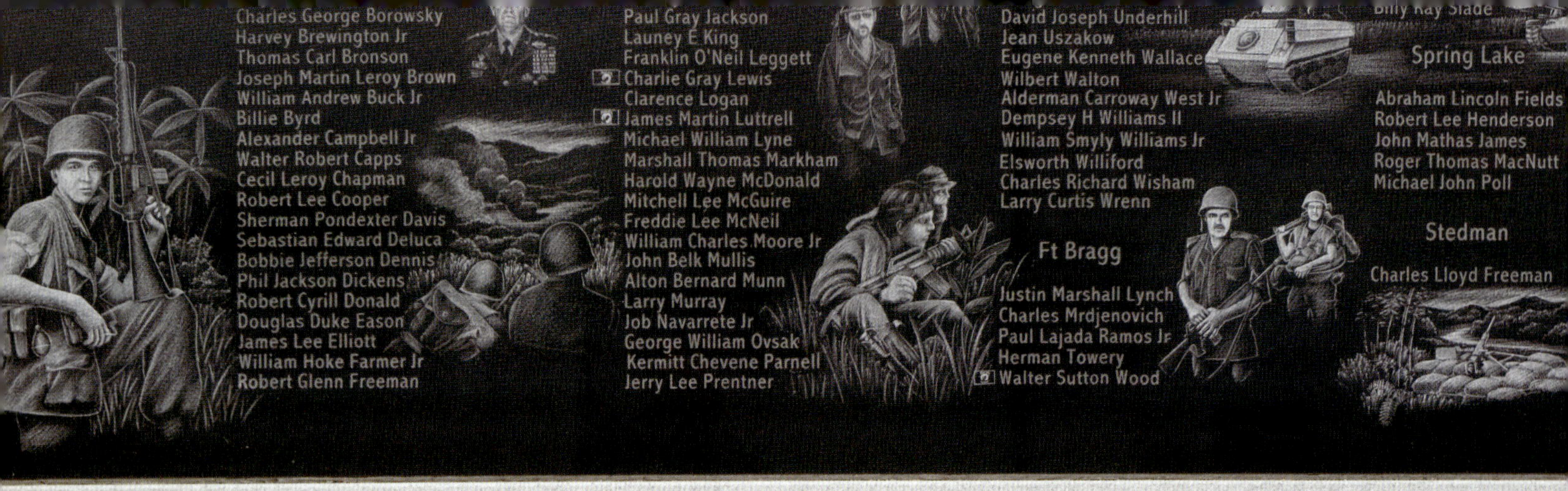

Photo by Alan S. Weiner

Let Freedom Ring

Located on the corner of Hay Street and Bragg Boulevard, Freedom Memorial Park honors the men and women of Cumberland County's armed forces who gave their lives in the line of duty. Monuments within the park contain the engraved names of those who fell during World Wars I and II, the Korean War, and the Vietnam War. In addition to public funds, the park, which serves as a gateway to the downtown area, was made possible by substantial contributions from members of the community. ✯

Photo by Shari Malin

The annual Operation Celebrate Freedom event that takes place each Fourth of July at Fort Bragg is designed to celebrate the birth of our country as well as honor our nation's armed forces. As expected, it can be an emotional event. Whether listening to a spirited song by one of the many music artists in attendance or observing the parade of flags from all fifty states, U.S. territories, and the units stationed at Fort Bragg, one is constantly reminded of the sacrifices made by those who serve. But there's also plenty of fun on hand, with food and craft vendors, carnival rides, and a big display of fireworks to cap the day's events. ★

Photo by Shari Malin

Photo by Bruce R. Feeley

CUMBERLAND COUNTY SCHOOLS:
A School System of Choice

"Our purpose is to provide students with the tools necessary to realize their dreams."

Serving fifty-four thousand students, the Cumberland County Schools (CCS), in Fayetteville, North Carolina, is home to eighty-eight schools—a combination of elementary, middle, and high schools, and special needs and alternative schools. In an increasingly diverse community, the school district serves the third-largest concentration of military-connected students in the world. One would think that the sheer size of the district and the frequent relocation of military students would present an almost impossible challenge. However, this school system can be described as superlative. With an innovative Governed Choice Program, in place since 1998, Cumberland County Schools offers all students the opportunity to maximize their learning potential. "Our vision is that the district will be a place where parents want to send their children and students want to come. Students who drop out often express feeling a disconnect between what was going on in school and what they were experiencing in life," says Bill Harrison, superintendent of Cumberland County Schools. "Our intent is to match a student's interests and learning styles with programs that keep them engaged."

The school district's materials describe the process this way: "How the curriculum is taught makes the difference. For example, if a child has special interests in technology, the parent can apply to a school where the curriculum integrates technology throughout the content areas. Not only would the teacher use technology in presentation, the student would also utilize a variety of technological tools in his work."

While adhering to the state's standard course of study requirements, the Governed Choice Program allows individual schools to infuse a thread of common interest through every subject. Schools must apply to participate in the Governed Choice Program. Those that choose to do so must prepare a proposal that includes staff and parental buy-in, supported by research and data that indicate the program's ability to enhance student achievement. "A school focusing on the arts would involve dance, music, and more of the culture and visual arts of a country studied in their social studies curriculum than would a school with a science focus," explains Dr. Lavetta Henderson, associate superintendent for curriculum and instruction.

Offering national and international models such as accelerated learning, International Baccalaureate, as well as career and technical academies, the district provides programs that will prepare students for the twenty-first century. "Our purpose is to provide students with the tools necessary to realize their dreams," says Bill Harrison.

In addition to the strong instructional program in the CCS, the district also has impressive extracurricular and cocurricular programs for students. Fielding more than thirty-five teams per year at each of the ten comprehensive high schools, athletics are an important part of the total school experience in Cumberland County. Along with the traditional sports, the CCS offers bowling and swimming. Other opportunities for student development include Quiz Bowl, Battle of the Books, Science Olympiad, Forensics, Orchestra, Math Counts, and more.

As children of military families, many students may feel as though they can't become involved in the district's programs and activities, because their families may be relocated. Cumberland County Schools will have none of that. As the first recipient of the prestigious

(Continued on page 64)

(far left)

Not only a presence around the world, the American soldier is also a daily presence in the Cumberland County Schools. As volunteers, supportive parents, and true partners, military parents are part of a day in the life of the Cumberland County Schools.

(below)

Serving the third-largest concentration of military students in the world, the Cumberland County Schools is proud of their award-winning JROTC programs (Army, Air Force, Navy) found in all of the ten comprehensive high schools. JROTC members receive recognition for scholastic excellence, leadership, participation in student government, athletics, and physical fitness.

Photo by Bruce R. Feeley

(above)

Developing the whole child means providing opportunities for healthy competition: Quiz Bowl, Math Counts, Science Olympiad, Battle of the Books, Forensics, Spelling Bee, juried art shows, and more. Whether winning with humility or losing with grace, competition in school prepares students for competition in life. Here, the South View High School Lady Tigers are winning the 2007 NC High School Athletic Association Girls' Basketball Championship, played in the Dean Smith Center at UNC–Chapel Hill.

(below)

The Cumberland County Schools provides academies in all of the high schools. From the International Baccalaureate to the arts, health careers to engineering, students can match their learning styles and career goals to a curriculum that prepares them for the twenty-first century. Here, an academy with a special emphasis on engineering and technology offers an academically challenging pre-engineering curriculum that includes robotics, pneumatics, and hydraulics.

(Cumberland County Schools continued from page 63)

Pete Taylor Award, given to the district for its strong partnership with Fort Bragg, CCS has programs in place to ease the transition for mobile students. Bill Harrison, regarded as a visionary leader across the country, serves on the national board for the Military Child Education Coalition (MCEC). He says, "Our military students face unique issues and fears. They understand personally what terrorism means. They know that their military parent may not be home when they return from school in the evening. Defending freedom is real to them, and that makes it very real to us. We need to do everything within our power to support them while their parent is deployed." Every high school in the district offers a JROTC program.

Students from CCS compete with students around the world for college admission and competitive scholarships. CCS graduates are routinely accepted in major universities and military academies. The Class of 2007 was awarded more than $28 million in scholarships.

To maintain the highest standards, the school district recruits faculty nationally and internationally, and offers employees ongoing professional development of the highest quality. Combined with a partnership with local universities and community colleges, this system's faculty and administrators come full circle to uphold the one motto that drives all initiatives—"We put children first." ✶

(above)

Incorporating technology throughout the district is a strategic priority of the Cumberland County Schools. Technology has changed instructional delivery, student engagement, data collection, and the operational management of the district. The Cumberland County Schools provides computer labs and access to technology in every school in the district, which enables students to learn valuable skills that will apply to their future school and work settings.

(left)

Great schools must have great teachers. The Cumberland County Schools has extensive professional development within the district to develop skills and enhance knowledge, which lead to a culture of sharing, support, and collaboration. From improving classroom strategies to technology to leadership development, the Cumberland County Schools is committed to doing whatever it takes to develop its people so that our children have the best in the profession.

All Photos by Bruce R. Feeley

Teaching and learning extend beyond the traditional methods in the Cumberland County Schools, where manipulatives and engaging activities contribute to the joy of learning. Diverse learning in a safe environment challenges students to explore and discover. Expanded literacy programs, inviting media centers, in-house student broadcasting stations, and computer labs across the district are examples of resources that allow students this opportunity. Rote memorization is replaced with exploring concepts and applying that learning to life. Here, kindergarten students are engaged in a lesson of creating words with magnetized letters and then writing those words on paper. ★

Challenging curricula, up-to-date equipment, and innovative practices all provide an open door to the future for students in the Cumberland County Schools. Here, chemistry students participate in the hands-on experience and teamwork that prove to be a winning formula for this school district. With a focus on rigor and a commitment to challenging students to achieve at their highest level, the Cumberland County Schools has seen increasing enrollment in Advanced Placement courses, and more than $28 million awarded annually in nationally competitive scholarships to its graduating seniors. The many accomplishments of students in the Cumberland County Schools indicate the successful approach of teachers who expect the best from themselves and their students while adhering to the mission of making learning an exciting and lifelong journey. ✶

Photo by Rod Reilly

THE BUSINESS COUNCIL:
Creating Strong Partnerships

> *"Small businesses are the backbone of the Business Council, and there isn't anything more critical that we can do as an organization than to help these businesses grow and prosper."*

With over one hundred years of successful history behind the Business Council, one might think that an organization with so many wins would not want to disrupt the status quo.

The Cumberland County Business Council brings new and innovative ideas and projects to this community every day through its efforts in economic development recruitment and retention, downtown redevelopment, business development functions, and unique military relationships.

The Business Council and its members are as diverse as the three hundred thousand residents of Cumberland County, yet they have a common mission "to improve the quality of life by creating wealth, jobs, and investment in our community."

As an organization and a community, Fayetteville and Cumberland County have been successful in these efforts through the creation of great partnerships forged with local government and other community organizations. One of the most visible examples of this success has been the revitalization of their downtown. Through the City of Fayetteville, the Business Council, and strong support from private developers and small-business entrepreneurs, residents and visitors can now enjoy a bustling downtown district.

"We researched potential projects that would have an impact on sparking the downtown revitalization effort," says Kirk deViere, a former chair of the Business Council. "These projects centered around driving investment through public/private partnerships as well as creating unique lifestyle workplaces and residential living. This spark created over $23 million in new investment into the heart of our community."

Storefronts have been filled with quaint and unique businesses, cars and shoppers line the streets and sidewalks, and construction projects continue to spring forth to further enhance a beautiful historic district.

The Business Council also enjoys a strong partnership with the County of Cumberland. Together they work closely on economic development recruitment and retention efforts. Through these combined efforts, the council has been able to recruit and retain thousands of jobs and create hundreds of millions of dollars in investment that might have gone elsewhere without the foresight of the area's leadership.

The Business Council has been involved in many collaborative efforts beyond the usual scope of a "Chamber," but it remains the cornerstone of the organization, with over thirteen hundred members. Their membership is built on small business, with traditional programming one would expect to find in a Chamber.

Over 85 percent of the organization's members are small business owners. Recognizing this fact, the Business Council has revitalized its small business effort to provide numerous training opportunities annually.

"The Business Council's leadership recognized the importance of small business and through their vision developed programs that would focus on small business growth," continues de Viere. "Small businesses are the backbone of the Business Council, and there isn't anything more critical that we can do as an organization than to help these businesses grow and prosper. Ultimately, their success is our community's success."

The Business Council is committed to working collectively with their many development partners in the community. Adds de Viere, "Connecting the dots between these organizations provides enormous thought leadership that facilitates the small business development and growth in our community."

The Business Council definitely proves that collaboration pays off. ★

(far left)

Lieutenant General Robert W. Wagner, commander of the US Army Special Operations Command, and Fayetteville Mayor Anthony G. Chavonne have an opportunity to talk one-on-one at the latest Military Affairs Council's Command Performance Breakfast. The event gives members a chance to hear firsthand what is going on at the base and how it will affect the Fayetteville community.

(below)

During the month of May, Fayetteville and Cumberland County recognize the importance of business and industry in the area. One of the most popular events is the Business Council's Annual Existing Industry Appreciation Golf Classic at Cypress Lakes Golf Course. Employees of local companies and members of the Business Council team up to enjoy the fine spring weather.

The Cape Fear River carves a liquid path through east central North Carolina. Born of the confluence of the Deep and Haw rivers just below Jordan Lake near the community of Haywood, the 202 mile-long river flows southeast and eventually widens as an estuary, emptying into the Atlantic approximately three miles west of Cape Fear. As the largest and most industrialized river system in the state, the river and its tributaries touch many lives in many invaluable ways. More than 27 percent of the state's population resides within the Cape Fear River Basin. Providing freshwater for businesses and residential uses, habitat for wildlife, recreational opportunities, and routes for waterborne transportation, the river is a vital natural resource. ✴

Citizens concerned about their city's environment and cleanliness formed Fayetteville Beautiful with the goal of implementing long-term solutions to maintain a litter-free city. Six subcommittees—beautification, education, communication, ordinance, enforcement, and technology—led by Bobby Hurst, Fayetteville Beautiful chairman, address individual behavior and boost volunteer involvement with the program. Here Don Jessup and Fayetteville children take a quick break from litter collection, as other volunteers continue the effort and beautify a roadside embankment with a planting. Using a Litter Index developed by Keep America Beautiful, the city can measure the success of its efforts, which have already resulted in the removal of tons of debris. All of Fayetteville's fifteen fire stations participated in this event, which involved cleanup efforts along sixty-two miles of highway. With red lights flashing, the trucks moved slowly through the streets, displaying banners that carried Fayetteville Beautiful's main message: "It Starts with You." ✴

Photo by Diane Kirkland

Photo by Bruce R. Feeley

Photo by Bruce R. Feeley

Photo by Bruce R. Feeley

Photo by Bruce R. Feeley

HOME BUILDERS ASSOCIATION OF FAYETTEVILLE INC.:
Helps Build A City

A booming housing market in Fayetteville maintains the health of this thriving city. That's why the HBA strives to advance the homebuilding industry through the promotion of new home construction and the support of housing-related professionals throughout the area.

> *"We are a large association of local businesses that care about the community where we live, work, and play."*

The housing market plays a major role when it comes to maintaining the health of a thriving city like Fayetteville. Recognizing this, the more than five hundred member companies of the Home Builders Association of Fayetteville Inc. (HBA) have dedicated themselves to keeping housing affordable in the town they call home, ultimately ensuring that Fayetteville continues to flourish.

"We are a large association of local businesses that care about the community where we live, work, and play," explains David Sykes, president of the HBA, which was chartered in 1963 to promote new home construction and encourage members of the local building industry to conduct themselves with the highest level of professionalism and integrity. "Keeping housing affordable creates job opportunities and growth for the community. Our industry supplies an enormous percentage of the workforce, and each house adds jobs and money to our economy."

Of course, the impact the HBA has on Fayetteville goes beyond economics alone. "Our members are community leaders as well as home builders," asserts Natalie Woodbury, executive officer. "We are hard-working people who care about the well-being and future of our area." That's why, in addition to being involved with fund-raisers and other nonprofit organizations, HBA members participate in a variety of community outreach initiatives, building Habitat for Humanity homes, constructing ramps for wheelchair-bound individuals, providing scholarship money at the community college, and more. For an association with such strong hometown values, it's just one more way to support and invigorate Fayetteville. ✱

Photo by Rod Reilly

Photo by Rod Reilly

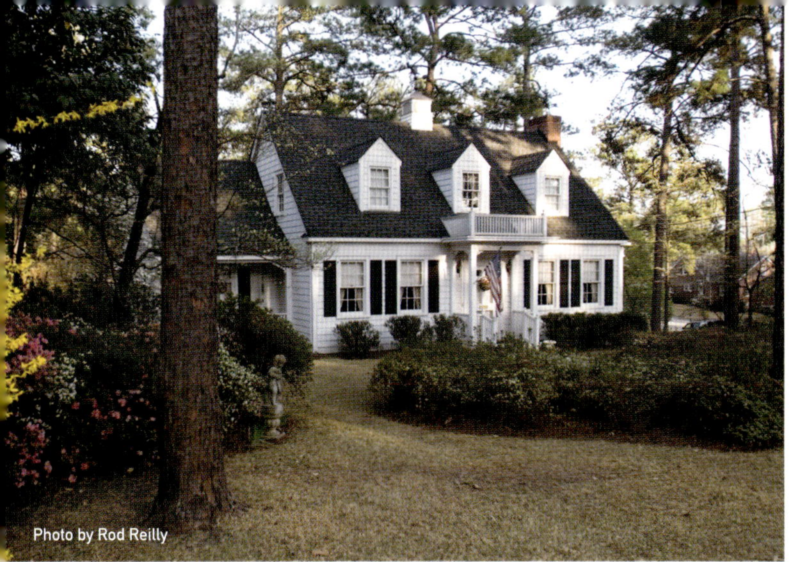

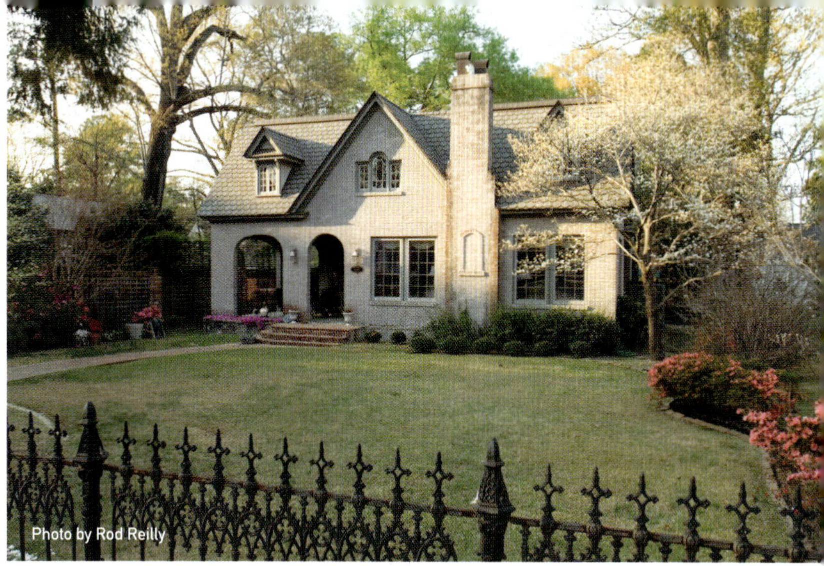

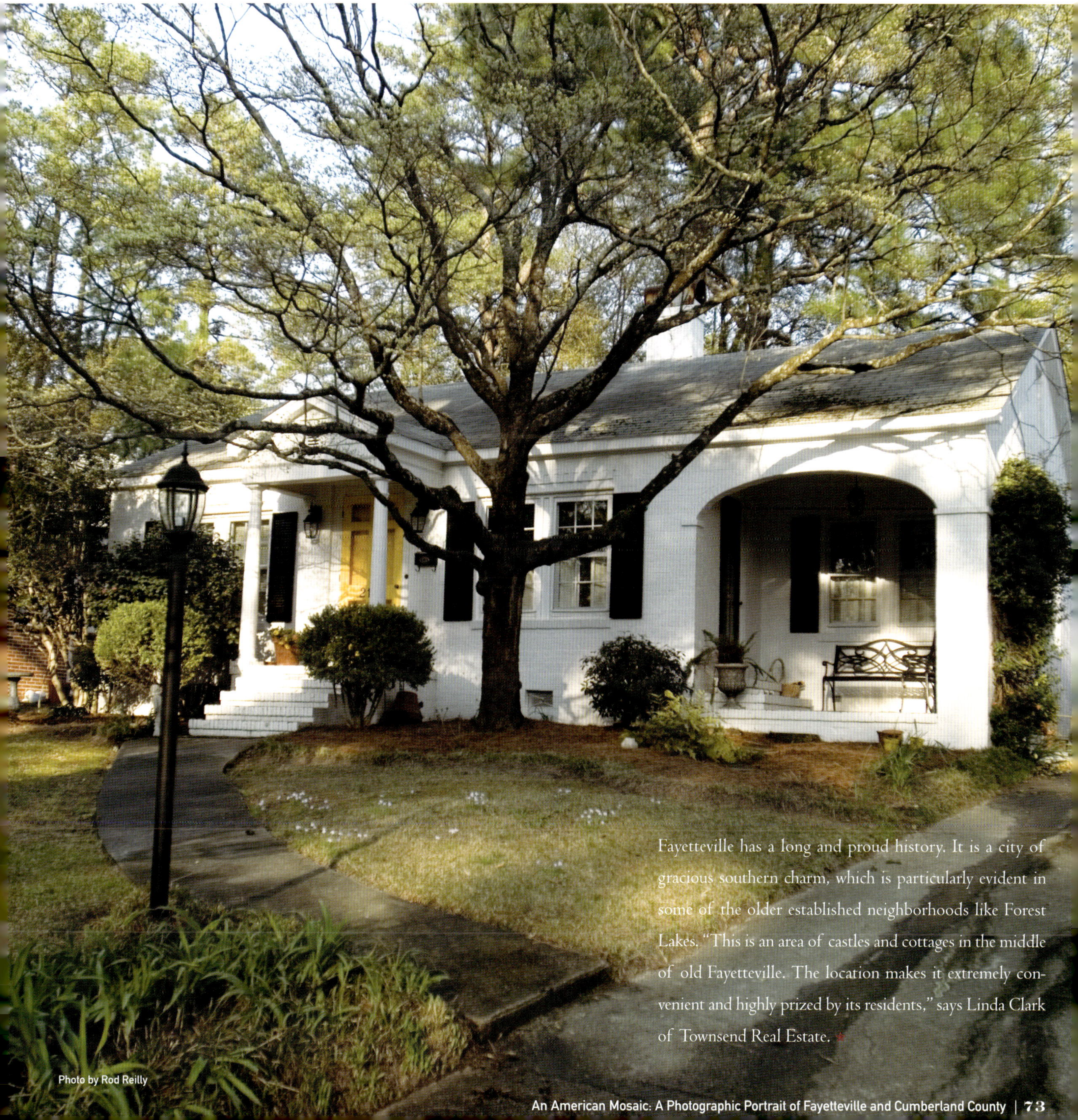

Fayetteville has a long and proud history. It is a city of gracious southern charm, which is particularly evident in some of the older established neighborhoods like Forest Lakes. "This is an area of castles and cottages in the middle of old Fayetteville. The location makes it extremely convenient and highly prized by its residents," says Linda Clark of Townsend Real Estate.

Photo by Rod Reilly

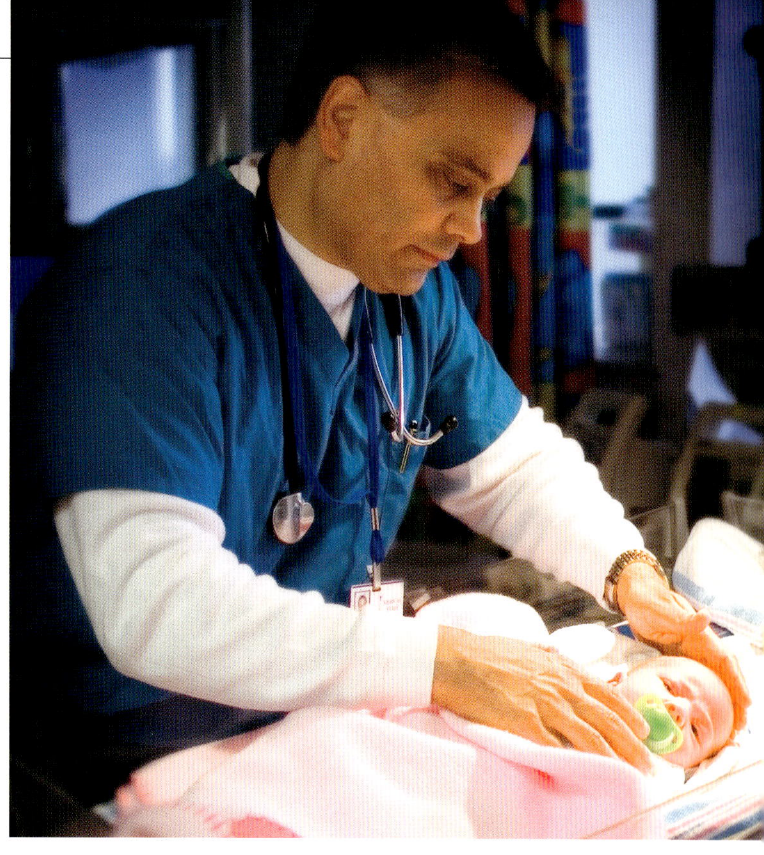

CAPE FEAR VALLEY HEALTH SYSTEM:
Expanding and Excellent Care for a Growing Community

When Cape Fear Valley first opened its doors in 1956, its founders wanted the new 200-bed hospital to provide the highest-quality health care possible.

More than fifty years later, that original mandate is still an integral part of Cape Fear Valley's mission statement.

Now one of the state's largest health-care systems, Cape Fear Valley has received several national awards and honors in recent years, which serve as a testament to that original thinking. The list includes Cape Fear Valley being named in the top 5 percent of all U.S. hospitals for overall clinical excellence and patient safety by HealthGrades for 2007.

To put the honor into better perspective, Cape Fear Valley is just one of three North Carolina hospitals to receive the clinical excellence award in 2007 and one of just six hospitals statewide to earn the recognition in the past five years. Furthermore, Cape Fear Valley is one of fewer than one hundred hospitals nationally to win both the clinical excellence and patient safety awards in 2007.

Other national honors include top 5 percent rankings for vascular surgery and pulmonary care and top 10 percent rankings for stroke treatment and bariatric surgery. Cape Fear Valley was also named Among the Best in the Nation for orthopedic services by HealthGrades.

And these numbers demonstrate service quality.

Medicare's most recent hospital quality comparison rankings, through September 2006, show that Cape Fear Valley is scoring above state and/or national averages on eighteen out of nineteen indicators.

None of these outcomes would be possible without the 450 physicians on staff, more than 4,000 employees, and the state-of-the-art facilities that offer technologically advanced treatment options usually found in larger cities.

Cape Fear Valley is a 619-bed regional health system and consists of four main hospitals that provide their own unique service to the community: Cape Fear Valley Medical Center is a 397-bed, acute-care hospital; Highsmith-Rainey Specialty Hospital is a 112-bed, long-term acute-care hospital; Behavioral Health Care is a 32-bed psychiatric hospital; and Cape Fear Valley Rehabilitation Center is a 78-bed rehabilitation hospital.

Housed within those hospitals are a wide array of specialty centers, including the award-winning Bariatric, Joint Replacement, and Heart & Vascular centers. The Cancer Center is one of the most comprehensive cancer treatment programs in the state, offering chemotherapy, surgical, and radiological treatment options, including Image-Guided Radiation Therapy (IGRT).

Cape Fear Valley's cardiac surgery program is now affiliated with Cleveland Clinic, named the nation's top heart program for thirteen years running by *U.S. News &*

World Report. Cleveland Clinic's heart doctors are pioneers. They invented cardiac angiography and developed the coronary artery bypass. Cape Fear Valley's cardiac surgeons are now credentialed by Cleveland Clinic and closely follow their award-winning cardiac surgery procedures.

Cape Fear Valley's focus on child health care is just as comprehensive, with a dedicated Family Birth Center, which delivers more than four thousand babies a year, as well as a Children's Center, Neonatal and Pediatric intensive care units, and a twenty-four-hour Children's Emergency Department.

In recent years, Cape Fear Valley began a multiyear, multimillion-dollar expansion campaign to better meet the needs of its growing service area. HealthPlex—a state-of-the-art fitness and wellness center that led off the expansion in 2000—is Fayetteville's largest fitness center at sixty-five-thousand square feet, housing two pools, aerobics studios with shock-resistant flooring, a one-tenth-mile walking track, and a full-court gymnasium.

(Continued on page 76)

(left)

Eugene Finch, M.D., a pediatric critical care physician, cares for an infant in Cape Fear Valley Medical Center's eight-bed Pediatric Intensive Care Unit (PICU). The PICU cares for critically ill children who require close observation and more intense medical and nursing care to aid the healing process. Patients come from many counties throughout southeastern North Carolina.

(below)

Cape Fear Valley Medical Center's Emergency Department sees approximately one hundred thousand patients a year. A new emergency department that is 33 percent larger will open in 2008 in the six-story Valley Pavilion.

(Cape Fear Health System continued from page 75)

Health Pavilion North followed in 2005 and quickly became the preeminent outpatient center in northern Cumberland County. Sporting modern and expansive architectural cues, the two-story facility houses its own pharmacy, family practice, and cancer centers, and X-ray, ultrasound, EKG, and lab testing.

Three ExpressCare facilities have also opened in recent years to help alleviate patient traffic into the busy Cape Fear Valley emergency department—among the busiest in the state. The first ExpressCare opened at Highsmith-Rainey Specialty Hospital, the second at Health Pavilion North, and the third across from the Cape Fear Valley Medical Center's emergency department entrance.

(right)

Health Pavilion North Cancer Center is the first facility in the Cape Fear region to have Image-Guided Radiation Therapy (IGRT), a new technology that helps patients fight cancer with unprecedented precision.

(below)

Patients and family members at Health Pavilion North Cancer Center can access books, magazines, and other materials on a variety of cancer-related topics in the center's Resource Room.

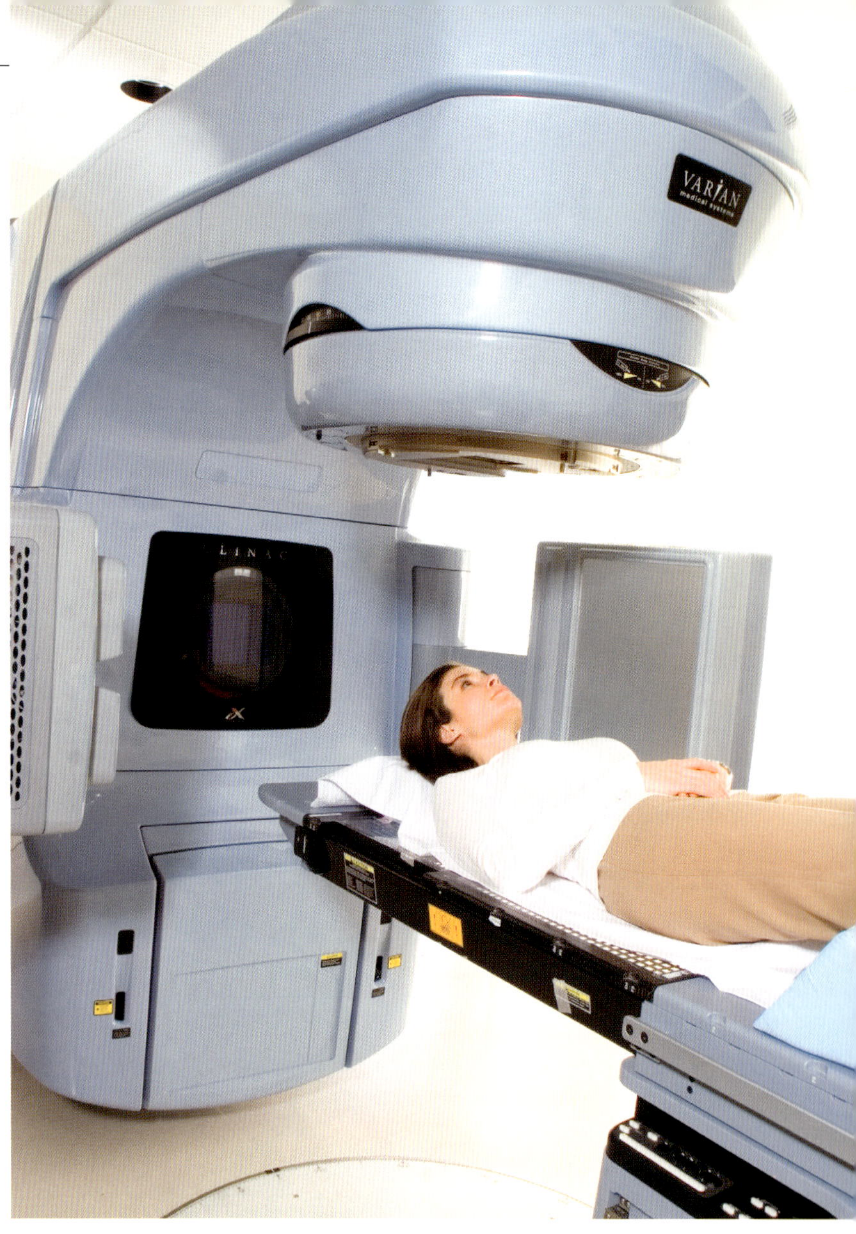

Efforts to better accommodate emergency patients will get an even bigger boost in 2008 when Cape Fear Valley completes expansion of its emergency department from fifty-seven to seventy-six rooms. The expansion is part of the Valley Pavilion project, which will include a new six-story patient tower on the south side of the Cape Fear Valley Medical Center campus. The facility will house 130 patient beds and allow Cape Fear Valley to centralize its Heart & Vascular Center. A five-story parking deck opened in July 2007 to better accommodate the growing number of visitors to the health system.

Such rapid growth may not have been predictable fifty years ago, but Cape Fear Valley's original mandate to provide the best quality health care certainly remains. ✳

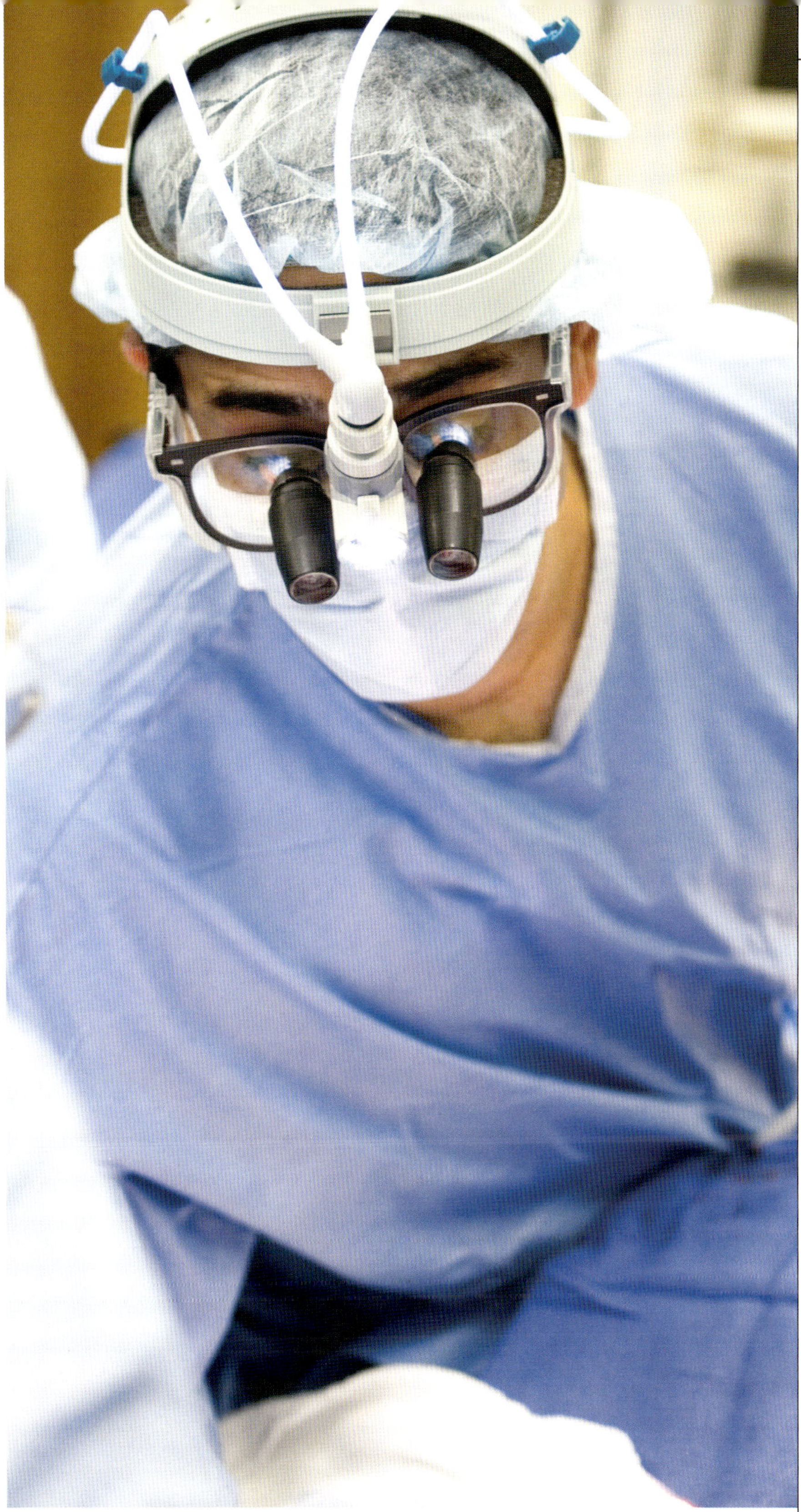

(left)

Cape Fear Valley's heart surgery program has partnered with Cleveland Clinic, which has been named the nation's number-one heart program by U.S. News & World Report magazine for thirteen years running. Cape Fear Valley's cardiothoracic surgeons will closely follow Cleveland Clinic's award-winning standardized procedures.

(below)

The flagship of the four-hospital health system, the 619-bed Cape Fear Valley Medical Center is a spectacular sight at dusk. It is easily accessible from the All-American Freeway as well as Business I-95.

Each year the Fayetteville, West Fayetteville, and Lafayette Rotary clubs join forces to produce the Annual Christmas Parade. "We want it to be fun for kids," says Johnson Chestnutt, "so we select a Grand Marshal kids know or can identify with, and we invite each elementary school in the county to select a child to ride on one of three corporate-sponsored floats." For the past five years, Johnson and Matt Smith have cochaired the parade committee. "We have about seventy-five kids on floats and another fifteen hundred students in the ten marching bands," says Smith. Add fifteen or twenty floats, live TV coverage, and seventy-five to one hundred volunteers on parade day, and you begin to see the amount of planning that goes into this event. ✯

All Photos by Bruce R. Feeley

OH WHAT FUN IT IS TO RIDE!

Photo by Bruce R. Feeley

ELMWOOD PARTNERS:
Their Business is Building Yours

At Elmwood Partners, finding the right commercial property starts from the ground up. The company was established by two of Fayetteville's most experienced real estate and construction professionals, Ralph Huff of H&H Homes and Tommy Bradford of Bradford Builders. Joined together as Elmwood Partners, the duo believes that the right property is key to a successful commercial enterprise.

As business owners themselves, Huff and Bradford understand that each venture is unique, encompassing not only what lies under the roof, but outside it as well. Their years of experience have gained them a sound understanding of all aspects of the commercial real estate market. Location, access, and visibility are therefore just a few of Elmwood's considerations when working with a client to design a property.

With Elmwood, Huff and Bradford bring their dedication and craftsmanship to large-scale, Class A commercial projects that provide their clients with the amenities to meet their business needs, and the Fayetteville area with projects that encourage revitalization and growth.

One such project is the Forum Office Building. The forty-four-thousand-square-foot, four-story Forum—the cornerstone of Breezewood Avenue's development as a bustling commercial center—will also serve as Elmwood's blueprint for similar projects, which Huff and Bradford are developing to meet Fayetteville's need for modern, large-scale commercial office space.

Other recent projects include the complete revitalization of a 1960s strip mall into the Elmwood Shopping Center, and the unique, one-stop home shopping concept featured at Showroom Square. With these and other projects, Elmwood Partners is proving itself a vital partner for Fayetteville's long-term growth. ✮

Location, access, and visibility are just a few of Elmwood's considerations when working with a client to design a property.

Photo by Alan S. Weiner

Holding Great Pyrenees puppies from Mom Maggie's ten-count litter is only part of the pleasure at Jambbas Ranch, a natural habitat in Fayetteville, as niece of the ranch's owner James Bass, Mary Beth Brock (left), and his daughter Jenny Carrol Bass can attest. This working ranch raises buffalo, deer, and elk and is home to llamas, farm animals, a camel, an alligator, and a bear named Ben. A one-and-a-half-hour walking tour leads visitors to a covered bridge, into No Chance Gold Mine, and over a narrow swinging bridge. Kids can pet and feed the smaller animals at this fun family stop that is open daily to the public. ✶

Photo by Rod Reilly

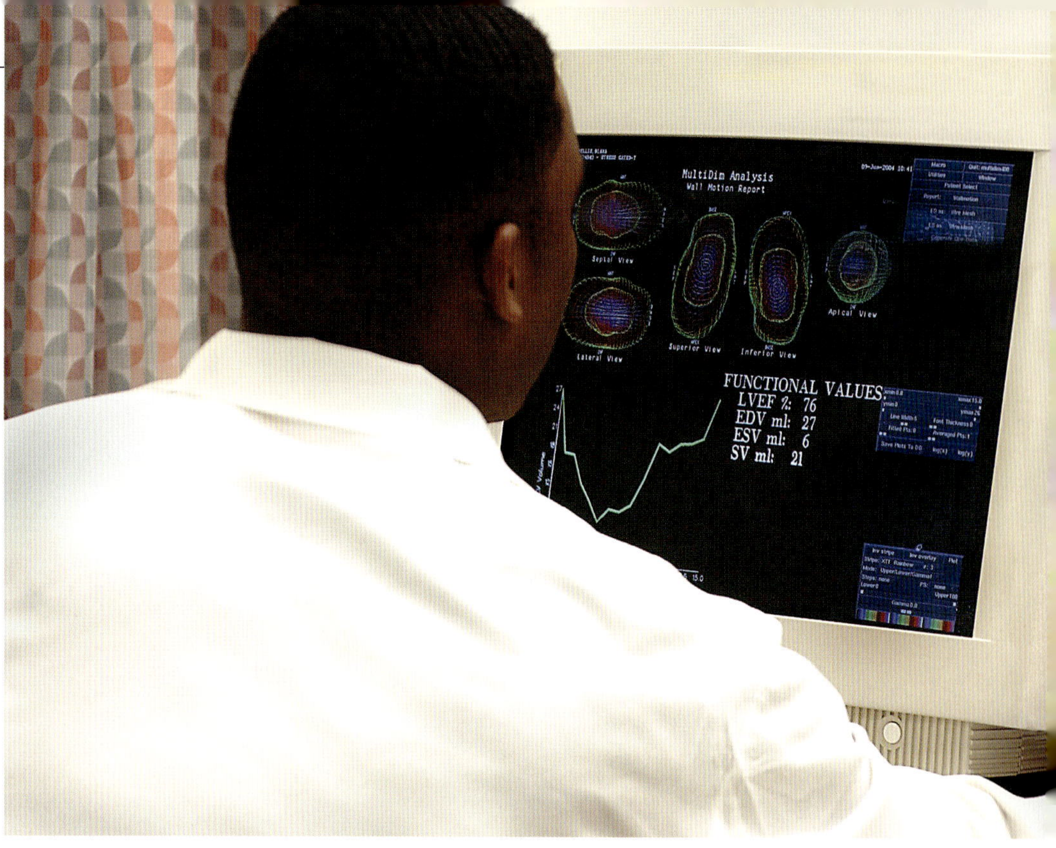

FTCC:
It's More Than an Education;
It's Your Future

FTCC provides a solid foundation of learning in the areas of business, general education, health care, engineering, applied science, and technology.

At Fayetteville Technical Community College, education is designed toward the career goals of tomorrow's workforce. Through certificates, diplomas, and associate's degrees in more than 120 areas of concentration, FTCC is meeting the ever-changing needs of individuals, businesses, and industries. Through its two-year associate's programs, many of which are transferable to four-year universities, FTCC provides a solid foundation of learning in the areas of business, general education, health care, engineering, applied science, and technology.

FTCC also offers certificates and diplomas in technical and vocational subjects that provide needed skills and training. From health-care emergency responder courses to programs geared toward office careers, FTCC covers the gamut of opportunities. There are programs covering multiple facets of construction, small engine and computer repair, culinary arts and food safety, and more—all designed to instill employable knowledge or help advance a career.

In its continuing education division, FTCC gears programs toward populations needing help with basic education, high school completion, or upgrading of occupational, vocational, or practical skills required for the world's rapidly changing environs. FTCC also offers noncredit classes for adults wanting to sharpen their personal interests, with classes ranging from painting and pottery to music and motorcycle safety.

Throughout the region, employers know FTCC as the place to turn for education of their workforces. The campus-based Center for Business and Industry through its business services area provides customized educational programs and training courses for employees of area businesses, government agencies, and health-care organizations.

In its industry training area, the center delivers employee-focused courses ranging from entry-level training for new processes or expanding business, to technical skills that enhance existing talents, to quality training in subjects like ISO 9000 and statistical processes. Industry training also tailors on-site retraining programs to employers' specific needs. Entrepreneurs turn to the center's Small Business Center Network for help with starting, developing, or growing a business.

A campus of great natural beauty, FTCC is home to the Harry F. Shaw Virtual College Center, which coordinates more than seven hundred online courses, and to the Horticulture Educational Center, featuring a 2,020-square-foot greenhouse and a floral design laboratory.

Accessibility is a key component to an FTCC education. The college's off-campus sites include Fort Bragg Military Installation, offering associate's degrees and continuing education courses; Pope Air Force Base, servicing airmen and their families; and the Spring Lake

Campus, an $8.5 million facility of nearly 64,000 square feet that holds thirty-four classrooms, twelve state-of-the-art laboratories, and a 102-seat lecture hall. Spring Lake also houses a North Carolina Information Highway classroom to provide for distance learning and teleconferencing opportunities.

Whatever the career, education, or training goal, individuals and businesses alike know that Fayetteville Technical Community College is a resource for a better tomorrow. ★

All Photos by Diane Kirkland

Every summer, Festival Park on Ray and Rowan streets in Fayetteville comes alive after five. That's all thanks to the Fayetteville Museum of Art, which annually presents Fayetteville After Five, a free concert series that attracts people of all ages to enjoy some great music under the stars. In 2007, the series attracted such popular acts as Wichita, the Craig Woolard Band, the Breakfast Club, and the Tams. And each year, the lineup just gets more exciting. Here, the green fills up quickly at 5:30 p.m., as local residents eagerly await the appearance of Better Than Ezra. The band's lively show was a big hit, as attendees enjoyed the tunes and the great company provided by neighbors and friends. ✶

PARTNERSHIP FOR CHILDREN OF CUMBERLAND COUNTY:
Making an Investment That is Sure to Grow

"I believe that no organization has the potential to improve the quality of life in this community more than the Partnership for Children."

Seated in kindergarten classrooms throughout Cumberland County are shining results of programs funded through the Partnership for Children of Cumberland County (PFC), a nonprofit organization that gives students a strong chance at succeeding in school and life. "Over the long term, I believe that no organization has the potential to improve the quality of life in this community more than the Partnership for Children," says Steven Moore, immediate past president of the PFC Board of Directors. "Setting up young children to succeed before they get to kindergarten will result in a better citizenry and a smarter, more competitive workforce. In my opinion, it is our moral obligation."

Established in 1993 to administer Smart Start, North Carolina's school readiness initiative, PFC builds partnerships with the community to identify and address the needs of its youngest residents and their families. "Smart Start is about personal and community participation in strategic planning, allocation of resources, involvement in decision making, accessing and/or expansion of community resources, coordination of special events, and an opportunity for political leaders to be informed and involved with policy development in the life of families who have children from birth to five years," explains Nae Headley, a PFC Evaluation Committee member and board designee.

The organization's mission targets four key elements of a child's life before age six: health; families effectively helping their children, including those with special needs, reach their potential; education and support for early childhood education providers; and support for organizations serving young children. In fulfilling this mission, PFC works with a comprehensive list of service providers whose expertise ranges from physical, mental, or developmental health to training in early childhood development to support the family unit. Beginning with only eight programs in 1993, the network of providers has grown to include thirty-two programs delivered by sixteen organizations today.

Board president Bishop Dr. Kenneth Hill believes this network strengthens the early childhood education system, a vital component in a strong community. "A better trained cadre of child-care providers directly affects the readiness of children entering the school system. Perhaps more importantly, it affects the rating of the community's child-care infrastructure, which has an impact on industry recruitment and enables more parents the opportunity to participate in the workforce."

In the 2005–2006 fiscal year the parents of more than four thousand children were able to work while their child participated in developmental and learning activities in child care because of Smart Start's child-care subsidy.

PFC's Child Care Solutions department works with everyone from families to policymakers to build high-quality child-care options around the area. For parents, PFC helps with the child-rearing process through activities like a child-care referral service complete with star-rated license information, access to background reports, teacher/child ratio numbers and other details about facilities, parenting workshops, child safety seats, a grandparents' support group, a resource lending library, emergency and crisis assistance, and more. For providers, PFC offers support services, such as grants, advocacy, start-up assistance, and training, in the area of early childhood development.

(Continued on page 88)

(left)

The Dorothy Spainhour Developmental Day Center serves children with and without special needs in an inclusive environment. The center encourages acceptance of all people and is funded with Smart Start funds by the Partnership for Children.

(below)

More Cumberland County kindergarten students are entering school ready to learn, thanks to the public and private dollars the community entrusts to PFC for investments in early childhood programs. Research shows successful early learning equals more success later in life.

All Photos by Diane Kirkland

(left)

Investments in high-quality early learning programs yield high returns for our community's economic future. Bank of America, one of PFC's many corporate sponsors, recognizes this connection and has contributed funds for us to participate in this publication.

(below)

Children learn through play in a More at Four Public Pre-kindergarten classroom at the Fayetteville Technical Community College (FTCC) Early Childhood Education Center. The center serves as a training facility for early childhood professionals and is funded in part by the Partnership for Children.

Photo by Diane Kirkland

(Partnership for Children continued from page 87)

PFC expands on the strong foundation for early childhood education established by Smart Start through implementation of North Carolina's "More at Four" Public Pre-kindergarten Program. This free, state-initiated program offers at-risk four-year-olds consistent opportunities to stay involved in high-quality educational experiences designed to help them succeed in meeting and maintaining the achievement standards established and expected for their age group.

"The More-at-Four program aids a child by providing more intense learning through play," says Monica Haynes, Child Care Solutions military outreach coordinator. "The programs provide developmentally appropriate materials and well-qualified staff to nurture the child's learning. Through these factors, a child in this program will have a better education and a better chance at success in kindergarten and beyond." Some 963 children participated in this program in 2007 at forty-nine sites in Cumberland County, including the Fort Bragg military installation.

According to the Business Roundtable, an association of chief executive officers leading U.S. companies, "In today's world, where education and skill levels determine future earnings, the economic and social costs to individuals, communities, and the nation of not taking action on early childhood education are far too great to ignore, especially when the benefits far outweigh the costs." Together with its community partners, the Partnership for Children is taking on this challenge and making an investment that is sure to grow. ✷

Photo by Diane Kirkland

Photo by Bruce R. Feeley

(above)

PFC's Omni Family Resource Center is a unique and centrally located home for organizations dedicated to helping families with children, both civilian and military. Forty percent of families using the center are military.

(left)

PFC's Resource Lending Library is a great tool for parents and child-care providers to bring different experiences to children. The library offers a wide selection of high-quality, age-appropriate toys, books, and games free of charge.

Important to all municipalities is a reliable collection service for solid waste. The City of Fayetteville strives to provide excellent waste collection service, just as crew members Veryl Flax (left) and Rosendo Vala are doing on one of their neighborhood routes. During the fall and winter months, the city also schedules free pickup of loose leaves, while year-round there is free service for picking up large items that do not fit in the rollout cart, such as appliances. A simple phone call or online request gets the job done for these special waste items. ★

Huell Akins is the mayor of Wade, one of nine municipalities in Cumberland County. (The others are Fayetteville, Spring Lake, Hope Mills, Linden, Stedman, Falcon, and Godwin, with Eastover expected to incorporate in mid-2007.) Akins is seen here in the town's new park, which has proven a popular enhancement to the town. The park was created with a ninety-thousand-dollar grant from the Parks Area Recreation Trust Fund, along with matching funds raised from among the town's citizens, who number fewer than six hundred. The park draws visitors from communities near Wade, and on any given day one can see children on the playground as well as young mothers with strollers and senior citizens ambling along the paved paths. ★

Photo by Alan S. Weiner

All Photos by Bruce R. Feeley

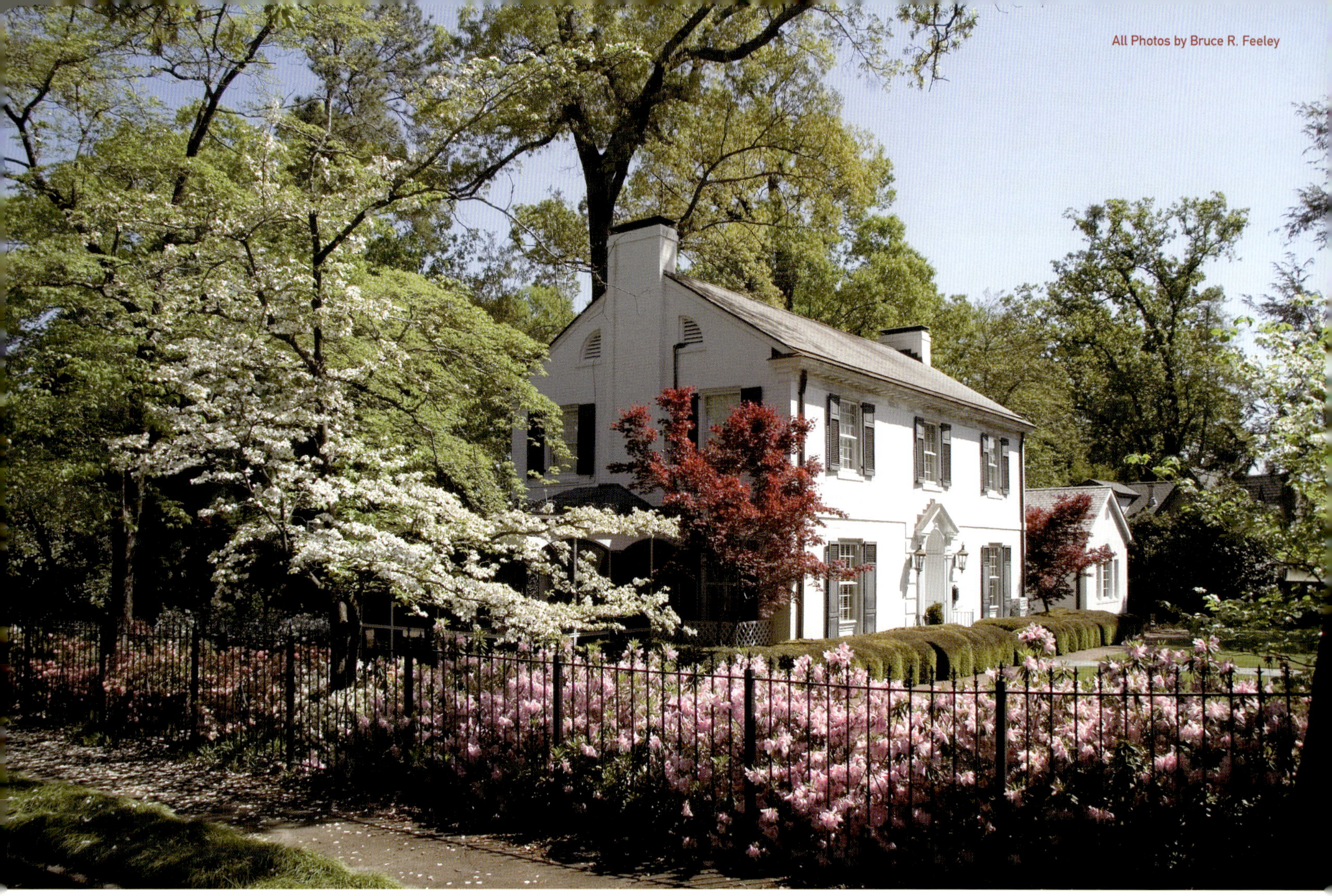

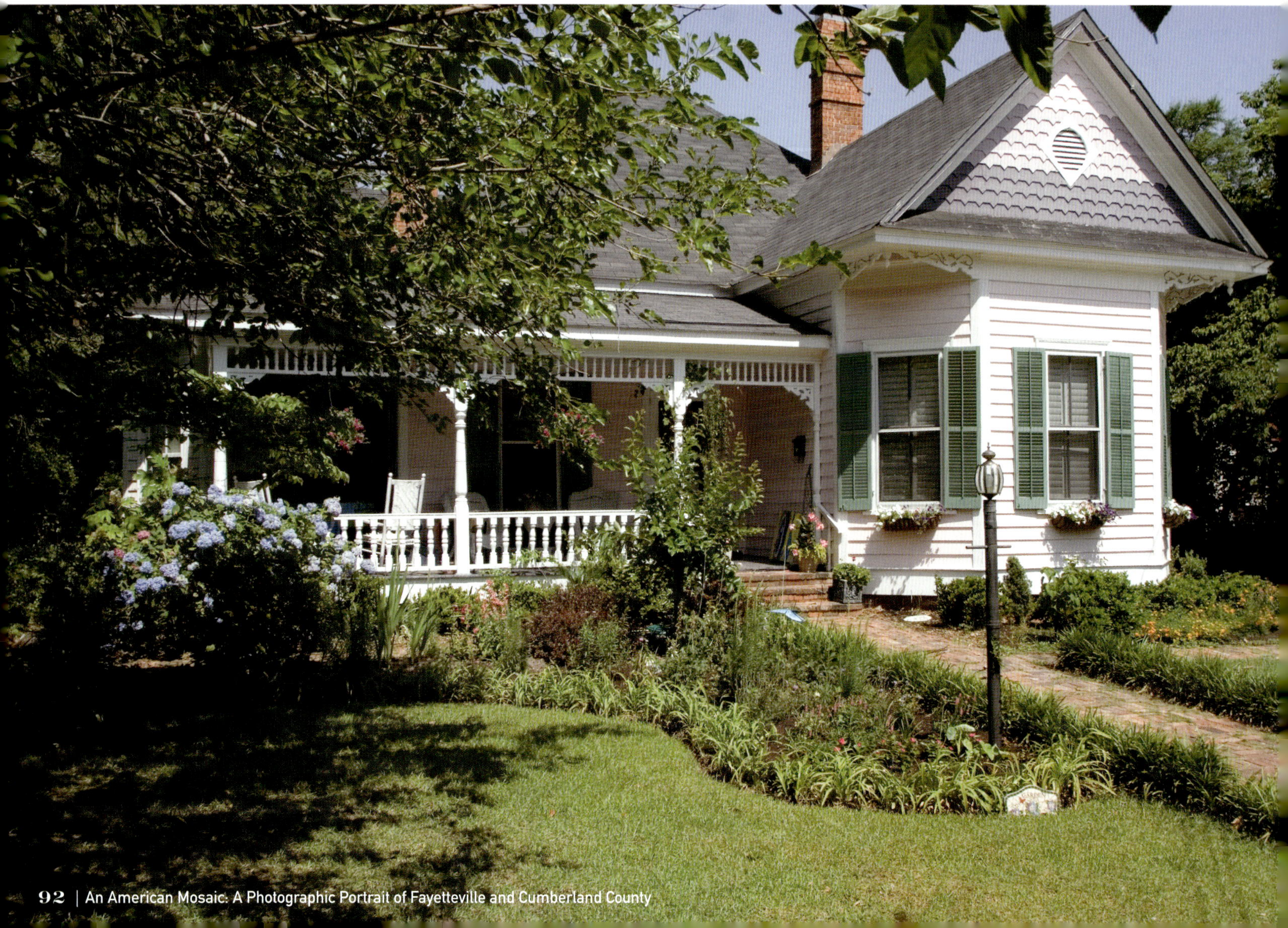

Whether "home sweet home" means a worry-free condominium, a new building in a gated community, or a charming older home with history like these lining Hillside Avenue, you'll find it in Fayetteville. In fact, the housing market is booming along with the rest of the city. By 2009, Fayetteville's population is expected to increase by twenty thousand, due largely to the needs of Fort Bragg. ✶

Plunge into summer by grabbing a Tarzan and trapeze swing or flying down one of a dozen different water slides at Fantasy Lake Water Park. Fayetteville may not have a coastline, but this six-acre, man-made lake does have a clean white-sand bottom and beautiful white-sand beaches. Visitors who are less adventurous can relax as they sit on the porch swings and dangle their legs in the cool water below. ★

And the Fishin' is Easy …

Located just off Belvedere Avenue, the Milton E. Mazarick Memorial Park is a popular recreational oasis. Named after a local Fayetteville businessman renowned for his community service and love of tennis, the eighty-acre park features a golfing area, softball field, playground, picnic areas, and tennis courts. Visitors can also spend time hiking the park's trails, or renting a rowboat to enjoy scenic and peaceful Glenville Lake. Surrounded by cypress trees, the lake is also a great spot to drop in a fishing line. *

Photo by Diane Kirkland

H&H HOMES:
Crafted with Care, Built for Life

Partners in marriage and in business, Ralph and Linda Huff understand the power of collaboration. It shows in the strength of their relationship, in the way they raised their two daughters, and in their highly successful home construction business, H&H Homes Inc.

The key to their success, says Linda, is to recognize and embrace each other's individual strengths. "Ralph is the vision; I'm the reality," she says. "Ours is a true partnership. He trusts me to do my thing, I trust him to do his."

H&H Homes was established in 1991 when Ralph, a REALTOR and former banker, decided to realize his lifelong dream to build homes. In 1994, Linda joined the firm as general manager. Ralph's prior experiences gave him a unique insight into the industry. But what attracted Linda, a former music teacher, to what she admits is a mostly male-dominated business?

"Well, I like challenges," she says, laughing. "But really, I quickly noticed that I was getting to work with some of the finest, most salt-of-the-earth people—the builders and contractors who put the homes together as well as the buyers."

Making those buyers happy is what H&H Homes is all about. "We never forget that every house we build is someone's home," says Linda. "We stress that with everyone we work with. If we lose focus on the people aspect of this business, then we lose all the way around."

Although he started H&H as a small, semi-custom home builder, it soon became apparent to Ralph that he should reposition his company to take advantage of what he predicted would be an unprecedented real estate boom. Sure enough, the boom arrived in Fayetteville and H&H evolved into a full-fledged production-oriented builder, but with the same attention to detail, quality, and efficiency that marked their custom work.

It's a combination that has made H&H Homes Fayetteville's leader in single-family home construction. So far, the company has built almost three thousand homes in subdivisions and residential communities throughout Hoke, Cumberland, Moore, and Harnett counties. Ralph chooses the lots and house plans, Linda and her staff oversee the construction details.

To meet growing market demand, H&H has also become a one-stop shop for the entire home buying process. The company's eleven-thousand-square-foot headquarters is not only builder central, but also houses its own affiliate mortgage company, real estate agency, customer service center, and warranty department.

Together, this team of professionals has dedicated themselves to the single task of building communities with quality, value, and integrity.

The Huffs are currently involved in developing nearly twenty neighborhoods, including two that feature a pool and clubhouse amenity typically found in upscale residential communities, but at prices that the average family can afford. They also utilize their expertise in developing several civic improvement projects, including a downtown mixed-use development, office parks, and shopping centers.

Generous contributors as well to a variety of community causes, the Huffs donate time and money to such diverse projects as local arts initiatives and the March of Dimes, from whom they received a Visionary Real Estate Award in 2006. The couple is also active in many civic and business organizations, such as the Cumberland County

(Continued on page 98)

(left)

He's the vision; she's the reality. Together, Ralph and Linda Huff combine their strengths to make their business all about the people they serve, from staff and contractors to builders and homeowners.

(below)

The Huffs have been involved in developing over thirty communities throughout our market area. Each is conveniently located near Fort Bragg, work, or shopping, and many offer pools, clubhouses, security gates, and homeowners associations to protect a buyers investment.

All Photos by Diane Kirkland

(right)
H&H Homes prides itself on offering innovative interiors in its models. Each H&H home bears the Huff trademark of quality construction, up-to-date amenities, and the comfort and warmth that make a house a home.

(below)
Fayetteville's growth naturally transfers into a healthy housing market. H&H Homes has experienced phenomenal growth from 75 homes in 2000 to 340 homes in 2007. Sales revenues for 2008 and beyond are projected at over $75 million annually.

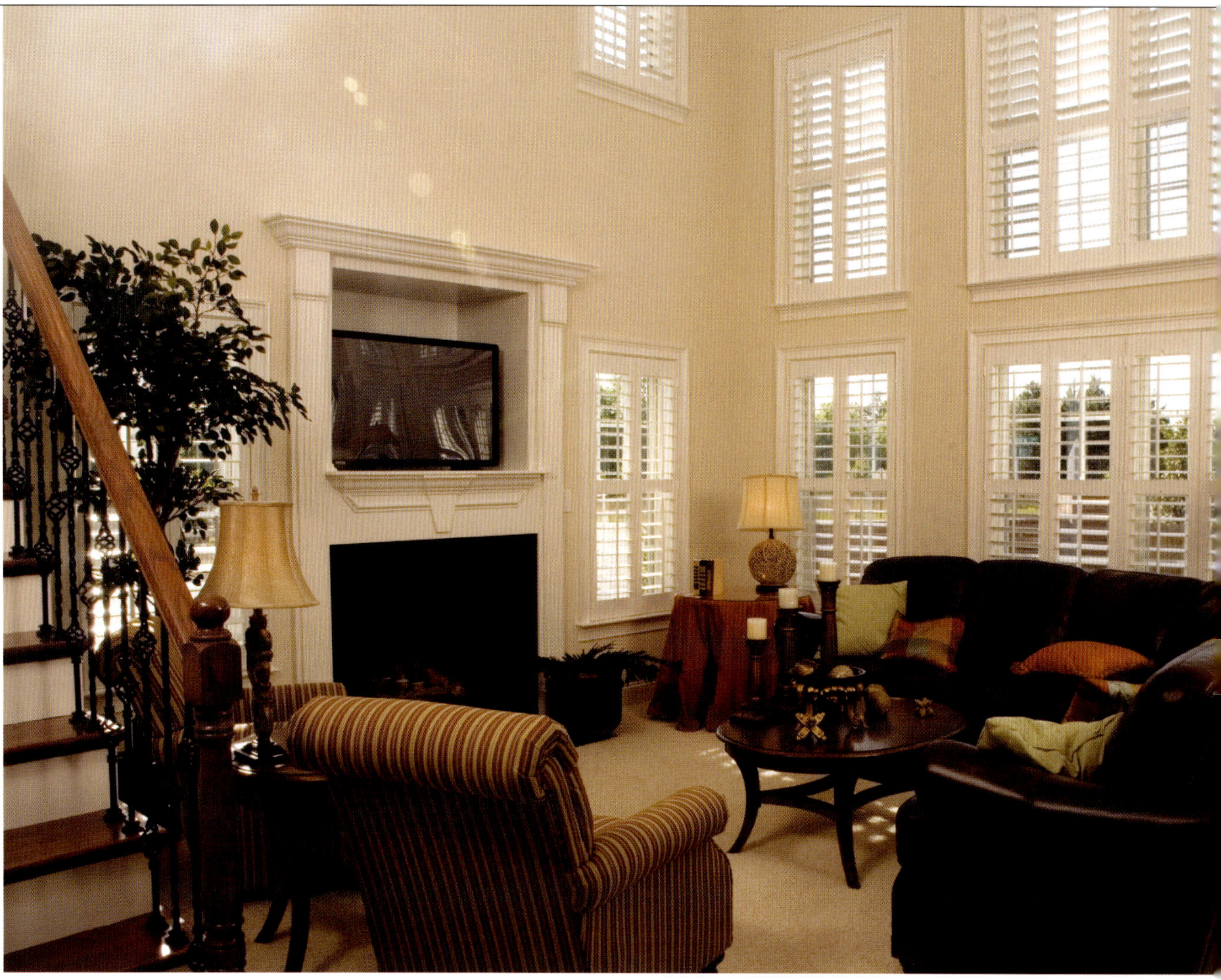

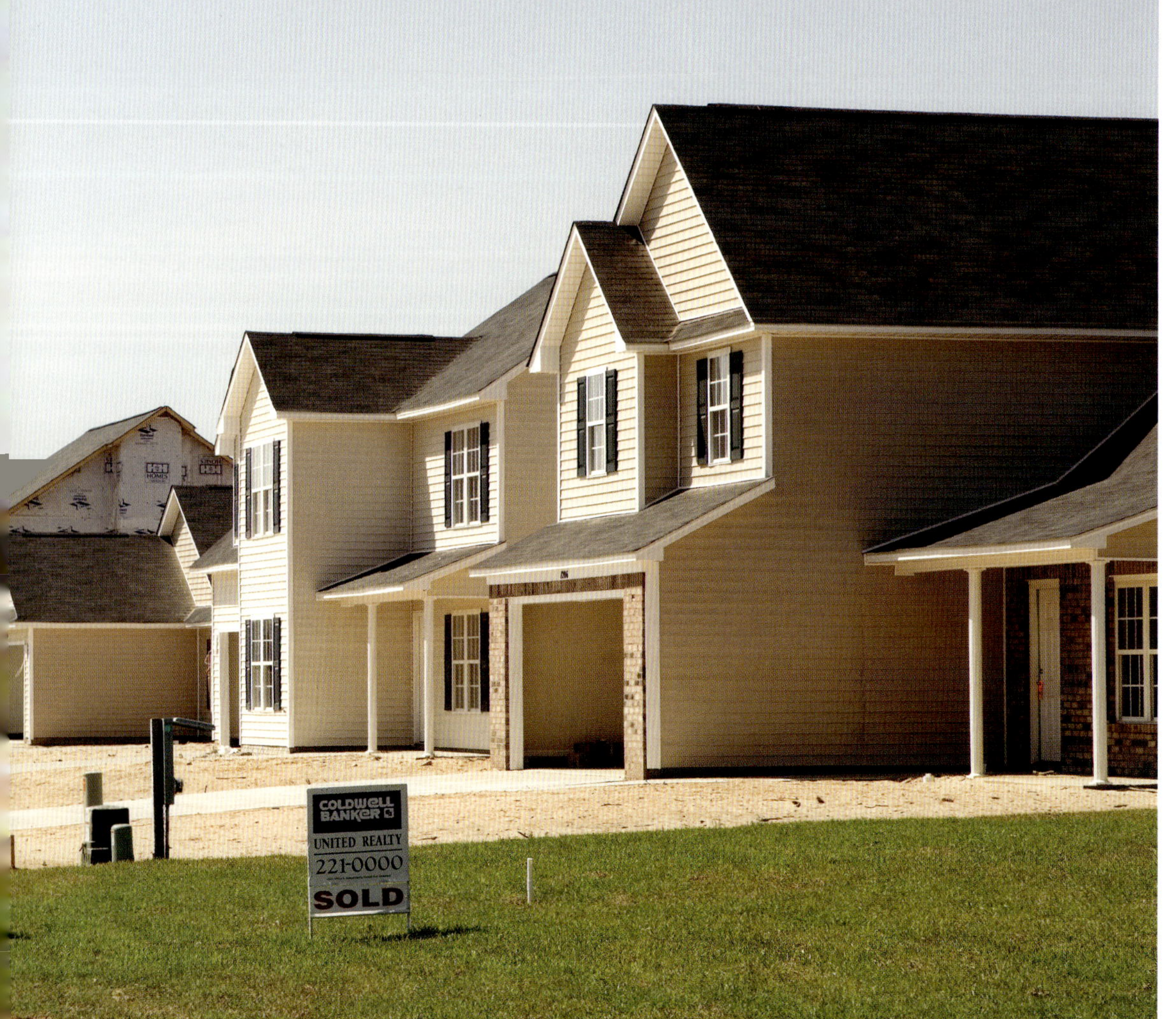

All Photos by Diane Kirkland

(H&H Homes continued from page 97)

Business Council and Fayetteville Home Builders Association, and they serve as elders and choir members in their church, First Presbyterian of Fayetteville.

With an eye, as always, toward the future, the Huffs intend to expand H&H Homes to all the counties that radiate outward from Fort Bragg. Says Ralph: "Homebuyers throughout the region should know that no matter where they are looking to buy, they have the option of an H&H Home." ✯

From its landscaped gateways to its downtown tree-lined streets to its parks and greenspaces, there's no denying that Fayetteville is a beautiful city. Maintaining the community's outdoor beauty is largely the work of the dedicated maintenance and landscape crews of the city's Parks Division. A typical landscape plan begins with design, followed by installation of irrigation systems and preparation of the planting area. Permanent trees and shrubs are then planted, followed by the planting of the annuals that add the bright color seen throughout the city. Here, crew supervisor Steve Morrison checks on sod prior to installation in a new park. ✷

FAYETTEVILLE PUBLIC WORKS COMMISSION:
Connecting with the Community

PWC has undertaken innovative projects to ensure the most efficient, cost-effective, and environmentally sound utility services for its customers.

Before the Civil War, water service in Fayetteville, North Carolina, consisted of hollow logs delivering water from nearby springs. In 1905, the Fayetteville Public Works Commission (PWC) was established to provide water, as well as electricity and sanitary sewer service. Over a century later, with the help of an archaeologist, PWC uncovered some of the old water-main logs and wooden reservoirs. They also renovated and landscaped the original well as a historic site. This project is just one example of PWC's continuing contribution to the city's history and development, in conjunction with their role as utility provider.

Throughout a century of service, PWC has undertaken innovative projects to ensure the most efficient, cost-effective, and environmentally sound utility services for its customers. PWC is the only municipal utility in the state to operate its own power plant. By generating power during peak-usage periods, the plant helps keep customers' rates among the lowest in the southeastern United States. Called a must-see operation by national organizations, this PWC facility was the first of its kind to boost efficiency with "combined cycle" generation. The plant also attracted worldwide attention for its innovative thermal energy storage system.

PWC has nearly six hundred dedicated employees who share the community's concerns. These employees live locally and work on the utility's systems every day, so when it comes to fixing problems, they're right on it. As a local, municipally owned utility, PWC's fast response time is one of its greatest benefits. This is particularly evident after major storms. If Fayetteville were served by an out-of-town utility, restoring service in this city wouldn't necessarily be that company's first priority.

For PWC, Fayetteville is always top priority. Residents have become accustomed to PWC's high standards for quality, reliable services, and those high standards have earned the utility national attention. In 2007, for example, PWC received the highest, Diamond-Level Reliable Public Power Provider national award for safe and reliable electric service. Since 2000, the EPA has honored PWC yearly with the national Director's Award for the Partnership of Safe Drinking Water, which recognizes utilities for going above and beyond in supplying clean, safe water. In 2005, Fayetteville won accolades for the best-tasting drinking water in the state.

Being part of a hometown includes community involvement and education. Two colorful PWC mascots—

Willy Water Drop and Wally Watt Watcher—visit schools and attend local events to teach children about safety and conservation. Long-term care of the environment is always a concern for the utility company. The PWC Watershed Program is the first line of protection for Fayetteville's water quality, as the surrounding wildlife and plant life play a key role in helping PWC monitor water quality. In partnership with the Cape Fear Botanical Garden, PWC also sponsors a "Water Wise" demonstration garden, as well as "Grinding of the Greens"—the annual program that recycles Christmas trees as mulch for the garden.

Dedication to a sustainable community was the impetus for a new PWC customer service center: a green building that will provide demonstrations of renewable energy sources. PWC also has a staff arborist who consults with homeowners about tree health, placement, and trimming options so trees can peacefully coexist with utility lines, while contributing to the city's appearance and air quality.

(Continued on page 102)

(left)

As Fayetteville's Hometown Utility, PWC provides excellent local customer service to over one hundred thousand customers each year and offers many options and programs to benefit its customers.

(below)

PWC is the only municipal utility in North Carolina to operate its own power plant. By generating power during peak periods, the plant helps keep electric rates for PWC customers among the lowest in the southeastern United States.

Photo by Alan S. Weiner

(PWC continued from page 101)

PWC's concern for excellent customer service is matched by its commitment to caring about its neighbors. The United Way has continually recognized the company on the state level for campaign support and volunteerism. Each year, hundreds of PWC employees participate in the local American Heart Association Heart Walk, helping make Fayetteville's Walk one of the most successful in the state.

Neighbors also have fun together, and you'll find PWC at most major city events. Thousands gather annually in the darkened downtown for the "Dickens' Holiday" marked by the grand illumination of festive lights, courtesy of PWC. Each year, PWC sponsors "It's Electric Saturday." This popular event celebrates the benefits of Public Power (municipal service

(above)

Customers can always count on PWC! Recognized for its high standard of service, PWC has received the highest distinction of electric reliability for national public power systems and is dedicated to always providing the fastest response possible to emergencies.

(left)

Committed to providing Fayetteville/Cumberland County with a plentiful supply of quality drinking water, PWC has been recognized for the highest standards of water treatment by the EPA's Partnership for Safe Drinking Water.

that operates solely for the benefit of customers, not shareholder profit) in a carnival
venue full of activities, including free rides in
a bucket truck. The utility company has even
put its support for the community up in
lights. Adorned with red, white, and blue
lights, the PWC water tower on the main thoroughfare to Fort Bragg is a proud tribute to its
military neighbors.

Established to provide utility services to
Fayetteville, PWC has evolved into much
more. PWC may stand for the Public Works
Commission, but the company and its
employees are also well known as the People
Who Care, thanks to the significant contributions they have made to Fayetteville's
quality of life. ★

Photo by Alan S. Weiner

Photo by Bruce R. Feeley

(above)
*PWC mascots Wally Watt Watcher and
Willy Water Drop make learning fun
while they educate children about utility
safety and conservation. Learning the
importance of conservation early on will
help shape future generations of responsible
consumers.*

(left)
*Initiatives to preserve and enhance water
quality include education through the
PWC Watershed Program. Educational
wetland ponds serve as a classroom for
demonstrating how plant life and
wildlife play a key role in monitoring
water quality.*

They sit straight with their feet on the floor and their eyes on the conductor. She raises the baton—and once again, they get it right! Hundreds of elementary school students who have committed themselves to excellence by devoting thousands of hours to study and practice become one wonderful orchestra as they perform before thousands in the Cumberland County Schools' Annual Spring Orchestra Concert. The Cumberland County Schools is proud of its commitment to the arts. Recognized for excellence by the Kennedy Center Alliance for Arts Education and the National School Boards Association, the Cumberland County Schools' arts program is vital to helping students improve their quality of life and develop skills that will provide beauty and pleasure for a lifetime. Music, visual arts, and performing arts are available to students across the district. ★

As a city of history, of heroes, and of a hometown feeling, the Fourth of July in Fayetteville is of course a special day. Celebrations run from backyard barbecues to neighborhood gatherings to gala all-day affairs with musical entertainment, laser shows, and fireworks displays. ✷

THE UNIVERSITY OF NORTH CAROLINA AT PEMBROKE:
A Personal Learning Experience

Tradition and the future . . . UNC Pembroke is focused on teaching and learning, and professors engage students in small classes. Undergraduate research, allied health and life sciences, internationalism, and entrepreneurship are keys for UNCP in the twenty-first century.

Students receive the personal attention they need to help them gain a depth of knowledge as they navigate a rigorous curriculum.

The University of North Carolina at Pembroke (UNCP) is where learning gets personal. It is a place where students become members of a community dedicated to providing them a foundation for success. From advisors who collaborate on initial course decisions, to academic tutors who offer an extra boost, to more than 250 distinguished faculty who take time to discuss studies and future goals, students are immersed in a world designed to make them competitive in the global economy.

With a student-to-faculty ratio of 17:1, and class sizes averaging thirty, students receive the personal attention they need to help them gain a depth of knowledge as they navigate a rigorous curriculum.

In addition to classroom studies, students learn by doing through the Honors College and the Undergraduate Research and Creativity Center. They conduct research, make presentations, and attend conferences, as well as perform internships and community service that provide opportunities for hands-on, demonstrable experience. In fact, about 90 percent of UNCP students are working within one year of graduation.

More than fifty-eight hundred students attend UNCP, enrolled in forty-four bachelor's and seventeen master's degrees in business, education, liberal arts, and nursing. There are also plenty of opportunities to participate in NCAA Division II athletics and more than one hundred clubs and organizations.

UNCP's campus is one of the state's safest and, according to *U.S. News and World Report*, one of the nation's most diverse. It is the perfect setting to turn learning into success. ✱

Photo by Diane Kirkland

Photo by Diane Kirkland

Each spring since 1984, the Cape Fear Regional Theater has taken a production to the great outdoors. The locale is the Campbellton Landing Amphitheater and the program is a lighthearted musical that is perfect for every member of the family. In 2006, attendees enjoyed the popular Smoke on the Mountain Homecoming, which was prefaced by an al fresco dinner before the show. Located on the Cape Fear River and named after the old ferry landing at Campbellton Village (established in 1730), Campbellton Landing "brings the people to the river and the river to the people." In addition to its amphitheater, which serves as a spot for year-round entertainment, the landing is also home to the Lord's Mill Restaurant and the Riverside Sports Center, from which visitors can purchase or rent hunting, fishing, and boating supplies and equipment. ✶

From Native American foot trails to horse, steam, and rail power, the history of transportation in Cumberland County is also the history of its position as a center of industry and commerce. With the opening of the Fayetteville Area Transportation Museum in May 2006, this fascinating history is brought to life through exhibits and artifacts covering such topics as the rise of the steamboats to Civil War rail lines. The museum's venue is itself a historic artifact: the recently restored 1890 Cape Fear and Yadkin Valley Railroad Depot. ✫

Photo by Erin Brethauer

Photo by John Chang McCurdy

Photo by John Chang McCurdy

CHOCOLATE LOVERS DELIGHT!

Michael Tallant keeps the windows at the Chocolate Lady sparkling so visitors can get a good look at all the wonders inside, where owners Jeanne and Bryan Nelson show off their array of delicious truffles. "We use no preservatives, and we make our chocolate fresh every day. That makes a big difference in the taste. Once you've tried our chocolate, you're hooked." Apparently, since a previous out-of-state customer ordered truffles shipped to Nebraska for her wedding. Plans are in the works to open a factory area where guests can see Jeanne making chocolate and a dining room upstairs that will feature desserts and champagne. ★

Businesses, art galleries, bookstores, and bistros . . . the only limitation on things to do in Fayetteville is one's energy to keep on going. Though Fayetteville retains a safe and southern flavor, this city doesn't roll up the streets at night. A recipient of All-America awards, Fayetteville's numerous daytime attractions are equaled only by its seemingly endless nightlife venues. Dance clubs, sports clubs, karaoke bars, live music, and over four hundred restaurants throughout the city entertain visitors to and residents of this sixth-largest city in the state. A downtown historic area (shown here) is the perfect location to take in a film at the vintage CAMEO Art House Theatre, to attend monthly open-air festivals, or to share a cappuccino or a glass of wine with friends at a sidewalk café. ★

Rude Awakening
coffee house
227
BISTRO
CAFE
cappu
open

Just Desserts Bakery
FAYETTEVILLE, NC
JUST DESSERTS
Bakery - Cafe -

Work

The diversity that has become so synonymous with Fayetteville and Cumberland County really does apply to all aspects of the area. That includes the city and county's thriving economy, in which businesses, organizations, and industries of all types and sizes have found a welcoming and fruitful home. And thanks to the healthy business climate that has developed here, coupled with myriad employment opportunities available to local residents, Cumberland County has become a truly superb place to work and build a career.

Now recognized as the "economic growth center of southeastern North Carolina," the county began its development as the Cross Creek settlement, where John Newberry built a gristmill in 1755 and essentially laid the foundation for Fayetteville's marketplace. While saw and gristmills were the main enterprises of that time, it didn't take long for resourceful and proactive individuals to become aware of Fayetteville and Cumberland County's potential, based in large part on its ideal geographic location between the Appalachian Mountains and the North Carolina coast. And when Camp Bragg and Pope Field made their appearances in 1918 and 1919, respectively, the local economic landscape quickly changed. Fayetteville and Cumberland County were soon bustling, with industries building up around the two military installations that today are known worldwide as Fort Bragg and Pope Air Force Base. And not only did the military presence pave the way for new businesses, but it also brought a new depth and breadth to the area's workforce, which is at once highly educated and skilled, as well as extremely productive. From students coming out of the area's superlative colleges and universities to exiting military personnel, Cumberland County's collective labor force is well trained, technically proficient, and thoroughly accomplished.

The uniquely balanced mixture of elements that make up Fayetteville and the surrounding metro area's business environment creates the perfect setting for a wide array of industries, from manufacturing and marketing to banking and real estate. The companies that have chosen to locate in Cumberland County manufacture products that are used nationwide and around the globe, and they provide high-paying jobs for the homegrown talent that is found here. They are as diverse as the people who keep them operating, and they are the driving force behind the continued economic progress that is certainly in Fayetteville and Cumberland County's future. ★

There's nothing ordinary about an ordinary day at Pope Air Force Base. As the day dawns, unit members are up and ready for physical training, which ensures that they are in top physical condition at all times. Then, highly skilled team members spend hours maintaining the incredible aircraft that the military depends on every single day. From the A10 Fighter to the C130, these capable individuals service and support some of the most sophisticated airplanes and jets in the world, caring for everything from their engines to their exteriors. And the work that they do guarantees that the pilots who take to the air in these magnificent machines can do the job they've been assigned to do. It's a team effort at every turn, and the men and women who constitute the various units of the Pope Air Force Base community always show great pride in the tasks with which they are charged. ✭

All Photos by Bruce R. Feeley

HOLMES ELECTRIC SECURITY SYSTEMS:
One Hundred Years of Service

Maintaining a successful company for one hundred years is a major accomplishment. Maintaining a successful family-owned and -operated company for that length of time is nothing less than amazing.

Holmes Electric Inc. was founded in 1908 by O. W. Holmes, who converted the trolley that ran along Hay Street to electricity. The present company, Holmes Electric Security Systems, still occupies the same block downtown on Hay Street.

"At one time my grandfather sold electricity to residential customers," said Stephen Holmes Wheeler, third-generation owner. "That's how it all began. Because electricity was so new back then, he had a shop at the front of the building where he sold lightbulbs and electrical items. Over the years, it became like a department store that carried gifts, household items, fine china, refrigerators, and televisions. We were the first Frigidaire dealer in North Carolina."

In the 1960s, as malls drew customers away from downtown, Stephen's father, J. D. (Luke) Wheeler, looked for other opportunities and created a new division specializing in security systems. In 2000, the company opened a branch office in Wilmington to serve the coastal area. When Stephen became president in 2003, he closed the appliance division to concentrate on the security and alarm business. Stephen's son Luke makes the fourth generation in the business.

Most people realize a monitoring service is the heart of any security system. However, many companies outsource that service to centers around the country, or even outside the United States.

"We pride ourselves on being hometown people serving hometown customers," says Stephen. "To maintain our high standards, in 1986 we created a central monitoring station right here in our building. We are the only security installation company in southeastern North Carolina that owns and operates its own U.L. (Underwriters Listed) central monitoring station. Our employees know the area, and they know most of our clientele. Customers aren't just numbers to us."

This kind of dedication extends to all services provided by Holmes Security Systems. Their installation services include burglar and fire alarms, camera systems, intercom and paging systems, and access control systems. Monitoring services cover basic monitoring by telephone line, long-range backup radio service, opening/closing reporting, elevator monitoring, and equipment supervision.

Holmes Electric Security Systems combines the best of old-fashioned service with the latest technology. "We keep up with the latest products, but before we install new technology, we test it in-house to see how it works. We don't sell out-of-the-box systems," Stephen says. "We listen to our customers and tailor our systems to fit their needs. We go the extra mile, like installing a system to monitor traffic flow or putting a camera in a high-theft area. No matter how large or how small a concern is, we make it our business to address the problem."

Training is another important aspect of security. "Our employees get both technical education and extensive on-the-job training to learn the Holmes way of doing things. We also train our customers, because the equipment is no good unless they know how to use it. We have staff here twenty-four hours a day to answer questions and dispatch technicians anytime they're needed."

(Continued on page 118)

All Photos by Bruce R. Feeley

(left)

Stephen Holmes Wheeler is president of Holmes Electric Security Systems. Stephen is the third generation of this hundred-year-old, family-owned and -operated company, which focuses on quality service to its customers.

(below)

Operators at Holmes Electric Security Systems provide monitoring for customers twenty-four hours a day at their U.L.-approved Central Station. Holmes is the only U.L. monitoring center in eastern North Carolina.

Photo by Bruce R. Feeley

Photo by Bruce R. Feeley

(Holmes Electric Security Systems continued from page 117)

Holmes Electric Security Systems is part of Fayetteville, not only in business, but also in community involvement. Over the years the family and its employees have served on numerous boards, provided funds for a variety of nonprofits, and supported the arts and education.

"We're proud to have been a part of Fayetteville all these years. We've grown and changed with the community, and we intend to continue to give our customers the best products and services for a long time to come." ★

When the North Carolina Public Works Commission purchased the city's venerable old Lafayette Hotel, it was with the intention of renovating it to its original purpose. But when the building caught fire, the commission decided to change its focus. Completed in 2000, the four-story, fifty-eight-thousand-square-foot Robert C. Williams Business Center not only houses the Public Works Commission's customer service center, it is also home to the Cumberland County Business Council, several law firms, a credit union, and various financial services companies. As a tribute to the Lafayette Hotel's history, the local architectural firm of Shuller, Ferris, Johnson, and Lindstrom, designed this stunning tower for one corner of the building. It stands as a modern-day echo of the original hotel tower, and pays visual tribute to the link between Fayetteville's past, present, and future. ★

Photo by Rod Reilly

NEIGHBOR HELPING NEIGHBOR:
The New Century Bank South Way

New Century Bank South opened its first office in Fayetteville in June 2003. The premise upon which the bank has operated since its founding is providing neighbor-helping-neighbor service to its customers. A member of the New Century Bancorp family, New Century Bank South established its headquarters in Fayetteville—a city "rich in history, heroes, and a hometown feeling," according to president and CEO William H. "Bill Hedgepeth. "Just the kind of place for an organization that is first and foremost a community bank," he says.

When New Century Bank South merged with Progressive State Bank in July 2006, assuming its branches and broadening its scope within the local community, the Fayetteville-based financial institution took measures to make its newly acquired customers feel welcome. But the endeavors were nothing out of the ordinary—it was just business as usual.

"New Century Bank South's mission is to be your neighbor-helping-neighbor bank," explains Hedgepeth. "As a community bank, we are committed to giving back to our customers and to exceeding customer expectations. We are here to provide solutions for all of our customers' needs, and we plan to do that for every customer who walks through our doors."

Today, New Century Bank South serves customers at six branches in Fayetteville, Lumberton, Pembroke, and Raeford. "The bank has experienced great success since opening, growing to over $199 million in assets in less than two years, due to loyal customers and an outstanding staff," notes John McFadyen, senior vice president and city executive officer.

That success also can be attributed to the full-service nature of the institution. Its extensive menu of products and services covers both personal and commercial accounts, affording customers a myriad of options from which to choose. "We want to meet the needs of the entire community, whether it is a small business loan for equipment, a development loan for a residential community, or a loan for an individual purchasing a vehicle," Hedgepeth asserts. Furthermore, all transactions are not only handled professionally, but quickly. He continues, "We are a locally owned and managed bank, and that gives our staff the authority to make a decision in a prompt manner. That sets us apart."

New Century Bank South's community involvement also makes it stand out. Volunteering time and making donations to organizations like the Cumberland County Business Council, the Kiwanis Club, United Way, March of Dimes, and Better Heath of Cumberland County, the bank has solidified its reputation as a dedicated corporate citizen. "New Century Bank South is a firm believer in contributing to the communities in which we operate," Hedgepeth maintains. And that philosophy is directly related to the purpose the bank strives to fulfill every day. Simply put, he says, "We are here to serve." ★

> *"As a community bank, we are committed to giving back to our customers and to exceeding customer expectations."*

The men who make up New Century Bank South's leadership team are thrilled to have the opportunity to help their neighbors in Fayetteville achieve their financial dreams. The team includes (front) William L. Hedgepeth II, president and CEO of New Century Bancorp and New Century Bank South, and (back row, left to right) Kevin S. Bunn, chief banking officer and executive vice president, New Century Bank and New Century Bank South; J. Gary Ciccone, chairman of the board, New Century Bank South; and John S. McFadyen, regional executive and senior vice president, New Century Bank South, overseas.

"Mangia! Mangia!" say Nick Parrous, Linda Parrous Higgins, and Tony Katsopoulos, the trio that runs Luigi's Italian Restaurant and Bar. Even though it would be seem more appropriate to offer the invitation to enjoy a good meal in Greek, as the Parrous family is of Greek descent, Nick says he sticks to the Italian phrases. More than fifty years ago, Nick and Linda's father Peter, a Greek immigrant, founded Luigi's out of a strong passion for cooking and love for people. The first Luigi's restaurant, a spaghetti house in downtown Fayetteville, served up Peter's mother's delicious red sauce. That recipe, and many others with Mediterranean-influenced flavors, have been favorites over the years in the many restaurants that the Parrous family has owned. "Your sense of taste and smell are deeply embedded in your long-term memory," explains Nick. "It's fun to replicate those flavors and create an experience for those who are eating." Luigi's current location has undergone several major renovations, the most significant of which came after the restaurant closed following the tragic murder of Nick's parents. Nick, along with sister Linda and brother-in-law Tony, decided to carry on Peter's passion and reopened the restaurant, which the Fayetteville community has always supported. ✺

All Photos by Bruce R. Feeley

Fayetteville Regional Airport ensures flight security with modern luggage screening technology. While interior upgrades have made the terminal a fresh, inviting place from which to embark on a journey, the airport property as a whole is involved in a twenty-year, $28 million plan of improvements that will ultimately result in a wider taxiway, rejuvenated tarmacs, reworked perimeter roads, and electrical component upgrades. ✮

CARPENTER, CAMMACK & ASSOCIATES/GALLAGHER:
Insuring the Area's Best

> *"Our job is to protect the assets, both business and personal, of our clients."*

Every business owner knows that adequate insurance coverage is vital to success. Ensuring that clients have the right products and services for their needs and exposures is the work of Carpenter, Cammack & Associates Inc., now a division of Arthur J. Gallagher & Co., the third-largest broker in the United States. "Our job is to protect the assets, both business and personal, of our clients," says Chris Cammack, president of the full-service agency that specializes in commercial insurance and risk management services, with their emphasis on medium- to large-sized entities.

Formed in 1992 by experienced independent agents Cammack and his partner Tom Carpenter, Carpenter, Cammack & Associates began as a three-person operation with a small office in Matthews and Cammack working out of his house for three years. Today, the agency employs nearly forty carefully selected professionals at offices in Charlotte, Fayetteville, Raleigh, and Greensboro; generates annual premiums approaching $50 million; and is associated with one of the top national insurance brokers in the nation, Arthur J. Gallagher & Co. Its product lineup has expanded to encompass virtually every major commercial property and casualty carrier, including Lloyd's of London and other international markets.

But while its offerings cover a broad spectrum, its service retains a personalized touch. "We take pride in offering comprehensive risk management services that can be customized for every business," says Cammack, who oversees the firm's Fayetteville operations with partner and senior vice president Mike Morketter. "We value long-term relationships with both clients and carriers, and feel that our reputation is the most important aspect of our business model. Because of that, from start to finish, we guarantee a professional, yet personal, experience that will leave clients feeling confident in their decision to choose Carpenter, Cammack & Associates. We like to view ourselves as 'big enough to do the job, small enough to care.'"

As part of its services, the agency provides clients and their employees with a variety of workshops and programs designed to improve the workplace and reduce insurance costs. "We know that companies which take a proactive role in managing safety and health issues in the workplace typically enjoy more productivity and pay less for insurance coverage," explains Cammack.

The agency also keeps costs low for their clients through its own efficiencies derived from technology; its client management system provides for a paperless operation and offers the agency's personnel ready access to client records with just the click of a mouse.

Because Carpenter and Cammack recognize that their own success stems from the trust others have placed in them, their agency gives back to special causes, especially those aligned with client interests. "The people in our office grew up in Fayetteville, so now, as business professionals, benefiting the surrounding communities is extremely important to each of us," says Cammack, speaking on behalf of the agency's personnel. "This is home, and we will continue to do everything in our power to not only provide services that will make our clients' lives easier, but that will also enhance life for our employees and our surrounding community as a whole." ★

(far left)
Carpenter, Cammack & Associates received the North Carolina Association of Staffing Professionals 2007 Vendor of the Year Award for its work insuring staffing companies such as Cape Fear Staffing of Fayetteville.

(below)
Mike Morketter, senior vice president, (left), and Chris Cammack, president, have served the Fayetteville community for more than twenty-five years, providing commercial insurance products and risk management support to businesses throughout the southeastern United States.

All Photos by Diane Kirkland

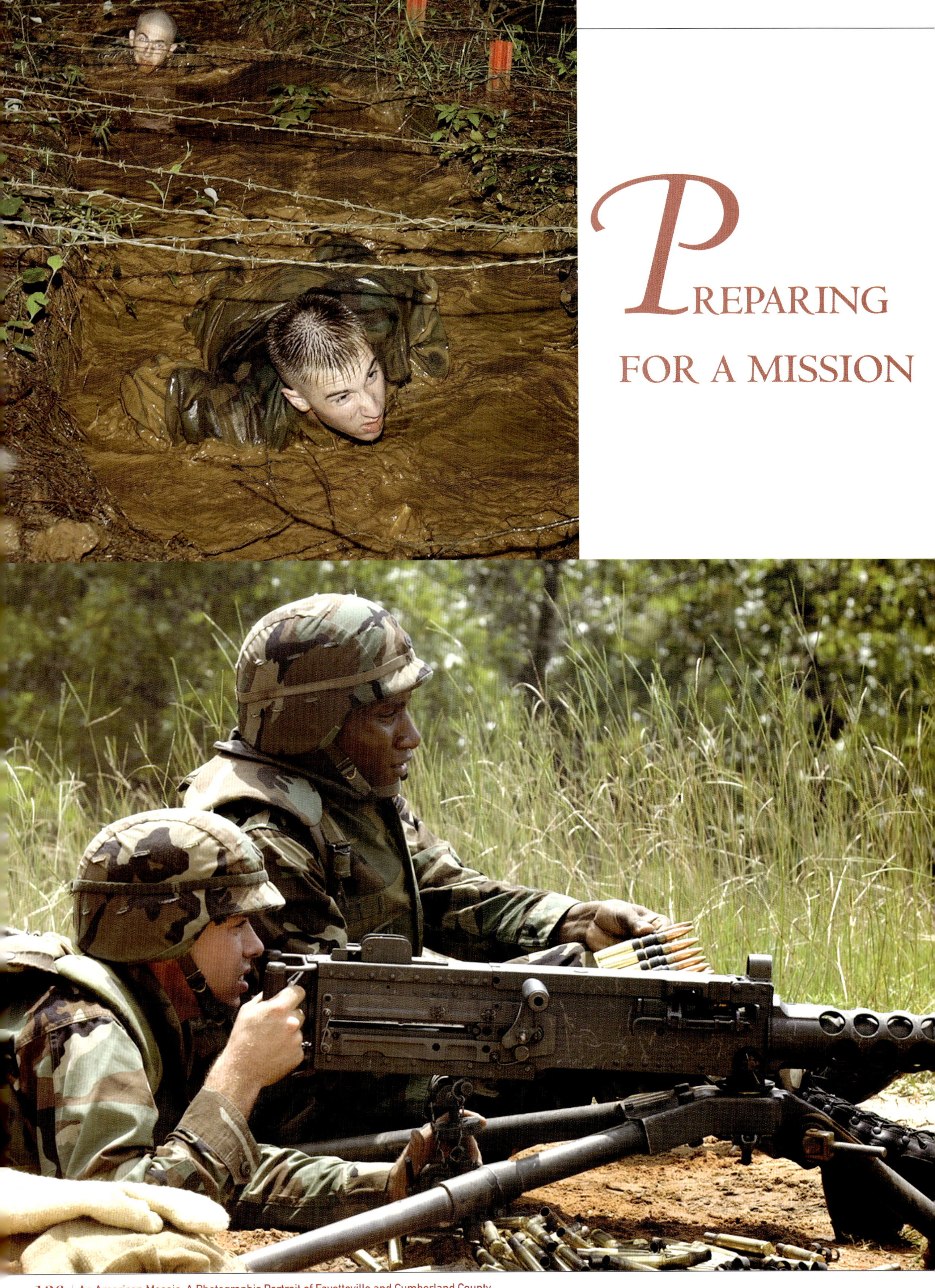

Preparing for a Mission

Photo by K. Kassens

The United States Army Special Operations Command oversees the various Special Operations Forces of the United States Army, consisting of Special Forces, Ranger, Special Operations Aviation, Psychological Operations, Civil Affairs, as well as Signal and Combat Service Support units, with approximately fourteen hundred soldiers assigned to each group. Highly trained, equipped, and organized Department of Defense forces conduct special operations against strategic or tactical targets during periods of peace or hostilities. The heroic troops of the Special Forces based at Fort Bragg arduously practice so that, when deployed, they are thoroughly prepared to conduct unconventional warfare and reconnaissance to support their country and fellow troops with actions such as guerrilla warfare, evasion and escape, subversion, and sabotage. ★

Photo by Diane Kirkland

HUTCHENS, SENTER & BRITTON:
"Doing What's Right"

"A major source of pride is not just our close relationship with our clients, but also how opposing attorneys, court clerks, and judges perceive us."

One of North Carolina's prominent legal practices, Hutchens, Senter & Britton, P.A., has prospered in its service to clients and the public at large by respecting the law and the people it protects, by understanding the dynamic needs of clients, and by consistently investing in the skills—and self-worth—of its professional and support staff.

Whether representing individuals with their personal injury, workers' compensation, or medical negligence claims, or representing business clients, the attorneys at Hutchens, Senter & Britton are the kind of professionals who do not just want to win cases. They also insist upon demonstrating integrity and fairness in dealings with others—in "doing what's right." These bedrock beliefs have set the tone for Hutchens, Senter & Britton's nearly three decades in representing clients and help explain its continued growth and success.

"A major source of pride is not just our close relationship with our clients, but also how opposing attorneys, court clerks, and judges perceive us," says partner Bill Senter. "They know we are knowledgeable, prepared, and honest, and they respect us for that."

Today, a staff of 20 attorneys and more than 150 support staff, including nearly two dozen certified paralegals, serve clients through the firm's offices in Fayetteville, Wilmington, Clayton, and Charlotte. Several traveling paralegals support Hutchens, Senter & Britton's ability and commitment to serve all one hundred counties in North Carolina.

At present, Hutchens, Senter & Britton's many practice areas include personal injury, workers' compensation, mediation and arbitration, medical negligence, catastrophic personal injury or wrongful death, creditors' rights, real estate and condemnation, business and corporate law, and estates and trusts. In addition to local businesses and individuals, Hutchens, Senter & Britton's clients include major North Carolina enterprises and a growing roster of leading national corporations, including those increasingly attracted to North Carolina's favorable business climate and way of life.

Under the direction of founder and managing partner Terry Hutchens, the firm has been instrumental in developing customized legal services for the real estate lending industry. The law firm of Hutchens, Senter & Britton continually strives to modernize its foreclosure practice by investing in new technology while respecting consumer rights and local protocol. The firm's stature in this area of the law is reflected in its membership and leadership role in the USFN, America's Mortgage Banking Attorneys®, a resource network serving the mortgage banking industry.

"Not only do we focus on providing excellent services and skilled advocacy to our clients, but we also are concerned about the well-being of our employees and the environment in which they work. We have a diverse, talented group of people, and there is strength in our diversity," says Rebecca Britton, one of the firm's newer generation of partners. "There's an emphasis within our firm for our attorneys and our staff to participate in community projects and causes."

Firm partners have always made it a point of soliciting ideas from staff members, whether toward organizing the legal practice, finding better ways to serve clients, or selecting community programs to support. This spirit of engagement is clearly evident in the participation level, energies, and overall enthusiasm that Hutchens, Senter & Britton people display in communities throughout North Carolina.

(Continued on page 131)

(left)

Whether welcoming individuals or corporate clients, receptionist Julia Smith offers a warm smile and assistance to guests at Hutchens, Senter & Britton.

(below)

(Left to right) *Partners Lonnie M. Player Jr., Joseph J. Vonnegut, H. Terry Hutchens, William L. Senter, Rebecca J. Britton, and John H. Britton. Hutchens, Senter & Britton insists upon demonstrating integrity and fairness in dealings with others—in "doing what's right."*

Photo by Bruce R. Feeley

(above)

Firm attorneys and employees participate in the March of Dimes Walkathon. Pictured are just a few who stepped up to support the community effort to save babies in the annual drive. The entire firm volunteers countless hours and supports local nonprofits, arts groups, schools, and universities.

(left)

Hutchens, Senter & Britton partner Lonnie Player (front) and attorney John Mandulak help fix up a Habitat for Humanity house for a local family during Law Day in May. Player is president of the Cumberland County Bar Association. The firm's attorneys serve on many local boards and are officials of state and local bar associations, as well as other professional organizations.

Photo by Alan S. Weiner

(Hutchens, Senter & Britton continued from page 129)

You may find Hutchens, Senter & Britton attorneys and staff members coaching football, singing in a local oratorio society, or performing at the Cape Fear Regional Theatre. The entire firm volunteers countless hours and is a continuing supporter of the community's nonprofits, arts groups, schools, and universities, including the Jimmy V Foundation Show Your Spirit Campaign, the March of Dimes WalkAmerica, the Care Clinic, Habitat for Humanity, and the Salvation Army's Coats for Kids.

Hutchens, Senter & Britton attorneys serve on many local boards, are officials of state and local bar associations and other professional organizations, and are frequent contributors to legal journals and continuing education programs.

"It's not just how we are viewed as lawyers that matters to us; it's also how we're viewed as people. We have a reputation for fairness and professionalism, and that, we feel, is the greatest measure of our success," Hutchens concludes. "We believe we reflect what is great about North Carolina and, in particular, Fayetteville and Cumberland County."

The creative, hard-working, caring folks at Hutchens, Senter & Britton would not ask for any description more flattering than that. ✶

Photo by Rod Reilly

(below)

Students from the 2006-07 Terry Sanford High School Mock Trial Team, 2007 NC State Champions, coached by HSB attorney J. Scott Flowers. Michael Koonce rises to address the Court. Seated team members, (left to right): Abhinav Kommandur, Ashley Arnold, Daniel Weaver, and Wynne Kelly.

Photo by Alan S. Weiner

(left)

(Left to right) Attorney Susan R. Benoit, supervisor Debra Milligan, and attorney Sarah D. Miranda meet to look over a case file. Twenty attorneys and more than 150 support staff serve clients through the firm's offices in Fayetteville, Wilmington, Clayton, and Charlotte.

Photo by Bruce R. Feeley

Early each December, loft dwellers in downtown Fayetteville open their abodes to visitors as part of the holiday event known as Candlelight Loft Tours. For a small fee, visitors can take a self-guided tour of a growing number of residences, most located in the upper floors of businesses in the area's renovated downtown area. Whether spacious or sparse, these homes give touring visitors an insight into the spirit of creativity and community in the city's core. ✶

Photo by Diane Kirkland

Sixteen feet tall and weighing in at more than three thousand pounds, *The Airborne Trooper* statue, better known as "Iron Mike," certainly stands up to its image. The term "Iron Mike" is American slang for one tough hombre and has become the name for many sculptures dedicated to our American servicemen. Sculpted by Leah Heibert and unveiled in 1961, this paratrooper has completed a jump into the war zone and is poised for battle. The sculpture guarded the front gates of Fayetteville's Fort Bragg, billed as the "biggest, baddest army base in the world," for eighteen years before being relocated within the camp. Iron Mike pays homage to all U.S. paratroopers past, present, and future. Due to deterioration, the original statue, which was constructed of polyester strips and epoxy stretched over a metal frame, was meticulously duplicated and replaced by a bronze version in 2005. ★

Photo by Rod Reilly

Mark W. Rice, president of Callahan & Rice, says the real value the insurance group offers clients is personalized service. "The key to our success is that we work with people on a one-on-one basis; you're not just a number with us."

CALLAHAN & RICE INSURANCE GROUP:
Covering the Community

In the forty years since its founding, Callahan & Rice Insurance Group Inc. has built its stellar reputation providing products for individuals and businesses alike in Cumberland County.

But its reputation stems from more than tenure, it comes from relationships with people in the community. One of the more visual demonstrations of the firm's commitment to the community is its downtown office, a structure built in 1900 that was renovated in 2006. Located just off the main thoroughfare, the building's revitalization has served as a catalyst for neighboring improvements.

While it represents a full array of intangibles, the real value of working with Callahan & Rice is found in its one-to-one service.

"Being active keeps our name out in the public, but it also helps people understand that it's not just about generating commissions; it's about making a better community," says Mark W. Rice, president, adding that the firm's involvement includes the Downtown Alliance, Cumberland County Business Council, the Fayetteville Urban Ministries, and Cumberland Interfaith Hospitality Network.

From this office, a dozen professionals, including founding member Thurston Callahan, deliver a lineup that encompasses property and casualty insurance, life and health insurance, employee benefits, advanced life underwriting, and retirement planning.

While it represents a full array of intangibles, the real value of working with Callahan & Rice is found in its one-to-one service. "We want new clients to realize that they are not just a number with us," says Rice. "They're not buying a piece of paper; they're buying a promise. Everyone should have someone they can depend on." Call Callahan and Rice today for your insurance needs. ✶

Visitors driving down Owen Drive may be taken aback at the sight of the Eiffel Tower, but Fayetteville residents will quickly associate this replica with the Bordeaux Center. Since 1963, it has been one of Fayetteville's favorite places to shop. In addition to restaurants and specialty shops, Bordeaux Center is described as "a planned professional medical community," conveniently located adjacent to Cape Fear Valley Medical Center. ✴

Photo by Diane Kirkland

TEAM HARRIS REAL ESTATE:
An Uncommon Vision

"We have a similar vision and mission, and that's to help as many people as we can realize their goals when it comes to homeownership."

Often, when a person takes over the family business from his or her parent, the new generation makes so many changes that the original version of the company fades away. Fortunately, that's not the case with Wendy Harris, who in early 2007 assumed ownership of the boutique real estate firm Team Harris Real Estate from her father, renowned Fayetteville REALTOR® Jim Harris. Instead, Wendy has managed to maintain her father's twenty-year tradition of excellence while taking the thriving company he founded to new heights.

"We have a similar vision and mission, and that's to help as many people as we can realize their goals when it comes to homeownership," explains Wendy Harris, now owner of the eight-person company. "My team and I are rooted in this community, and we provide an unparalleled level of personalized service to our customers."

Residents of Fayetteville since the early 1980s, the Harrises have a great deal of knowledge about the area, which includes the key military installation Fort Bragg. Team Harris has been able to use that wisdom to carve out a niche in the market, working with military families to help them find homes when they arrive in Fayetteville to serve at Fort Bragg. They even travel around the country annually to various military bases so she can make contact with people who likely will be transferred to Fort Bragg, giving them a head start on their move. "We love our troops, and we appreciate their sacrifices for our country," she declares. "We go above and beyond to make their transition to our community a seamless one. We want every newcomer to love it here as much as we do."

This credo also applies to the firm's many civilian home buyers and home sellers. That's why Team Harris offers a variety of value-added services for past and present clients, such as access to a moving truck, a key cutting machine, an annual investment analysis, and a client-for-life program. Additionally, the company is strategically structured to make the process of buying or selling a home as efficient and easy for everyone involved. "Every team member is fully cross-trained in all areas, but each team member specializes," Harris notes.

For instance, there are agents who have special expertise with buyers, new construction, farms, and equestrian properties, to name a few; Harris herself specializes in listings and marketing. The firm also has administrative professionals who handle the closing and marketing processes, and another who spearheads the team's community involvement initiatives. "It's hard for one person to be an expert at everything," she adds. "This is why Team Harris is designed to work as a team, and it makes us stronger and better."

It also sets Team Harris apart—not only within the real estate industry, but also the local community. Then again, with Harris and her team, which still includes Jim, working together for military-civilian organizations and groups like Leadership Fayetteville, it's not hard to stand out. And it's the team's camaraderie—and family spirit—that allows Team Harris Real Estate to serve its clients and its hometown so well. ★

Photo by John Chang McCurdy

To counteract an annual antiwar event, many Fayetteville citizens held a Support the Troops Rally. The crowd waved flags, held posters, and verbally stated their allegiance to the thousands of troops and their families based at nearby Fort Bragg and Pope Air Force Base, as well as the troops engaged in Iraq and Afghanistan. Joining in the patriotic rally were representatives of the Freerepublic Network, Carolina Support the Troops, families of veterans, relatives of World Trade Center victims, Veterans of Foreign Wars, and active military personnel. Early in 2007, nine paratroopers from Fort Bragg's Airborne Unit lost their lives to a suicide bomber in Iraq, bringing the loss from that division to more than one hundred who have bravely sacrificed their lives for their country. ✸

Photo by Rod Reilly

Photo by Rod Reilly

Photo by Rod Reilly

COLDWELL BANKER UNITED REALTY:
Recognized Worldwide

"We are the most successful office of our size in the southern region of Coldwell Banker."

Not only is it known worldwide, but approximately one in every ten home sales in the United States that uses a real estate agency involves a Coldwell Banker sales associate. "Ironically that's true for Coldwell Banker United Realty here in Fayetteville too," said Greg West, general manager.

"Our local clients get the backing of Coldwell Banker's one-hundred-year history, plus the advantage of dealing with an independently owned agency staffed by full-time associates who know the area because we live here."

United Realty has served the Fayetteville community since 1970. The firm stands out from the competition because it is a balanced brokerage which represents a wide array of new construction, as well as resale of existing homes and relocation, which deals with incoming buyers. "We are the most successful office of our size in the southern region of Coldwell Banker, an area that covers fourteen states from North Carolina to Texas."

Coldwell Banker United Realty has been designated a Premier Office every year since 1991. It recently received the President's Circle Award, given to only a handful of offices nationwide.

"We're equally proud that we've stayed on top," West continued. The Fayetteville location completes sixteen hundred transactions a year, more than twice the number for a typical real estate office of its size.

Part of this success is attributed to United Realty's use of technology to enhance customer service. Today more than 80 percent of potential movers begin their search online, and www.coldwellbanker.com is one of the leading national real estate Web sites. "To serve clients better, we established www.cburhomes.com, which supplies a wealth of relevant information, virtual tours, and no fewer than six photographs for each listing," explained West.

Because buying or selling a home can be complicated, the company is always looking for ways technology can make the process easier. "We work hard to make sure each transaction goes smoothly. That's especially true with our military clients around the world."

Because Coldwell Banker has associates throughout the United States, as well as in Canada, Europe, Puerto Rico, Mexico, the Philippines, Bermuda, Israel, Singapore, Central America, China, and the Caribbean, a move necessitated by a new assignment can be handled quickly and smoothly. "We've learned from dealing with clients at Fort Bragg that decisions often have to be made by the remaining spouse after the person on active duty is deployed," West said.

Because United Realty agents and staff are area residents, they are always working to make the Fayetteville community better. They commit their time and money to various churches and organizations. The firm traditionally supports the March of Dimes WalkAmerica and Habitat for Humanity, and is proud of its 100 percent participation in the annual United Way campaign.

"Every day our agents are on the front lines being ambassadors for all that is great about Fayetteville and the surrounding communities," said West. "It's just a natural part of what we do." ★

(far left)
Coldwell Banker United Realty takes pride in serving those who serve our country. Agents receive special training to ensure a smooth transaction for those transferring to and from the Fayetteville/Fort Bragg area.

(below)
Coldwell Banker is nationally recognized for its professionalism and commitment to home ownership. For over thirty-seven years, the experienced agents of Coldwell Banker United Realty have worked diligently to help customers secure a piece of the American dream.

All Photos by Diane Kirkland

All Photos by Bruce R. Feeley

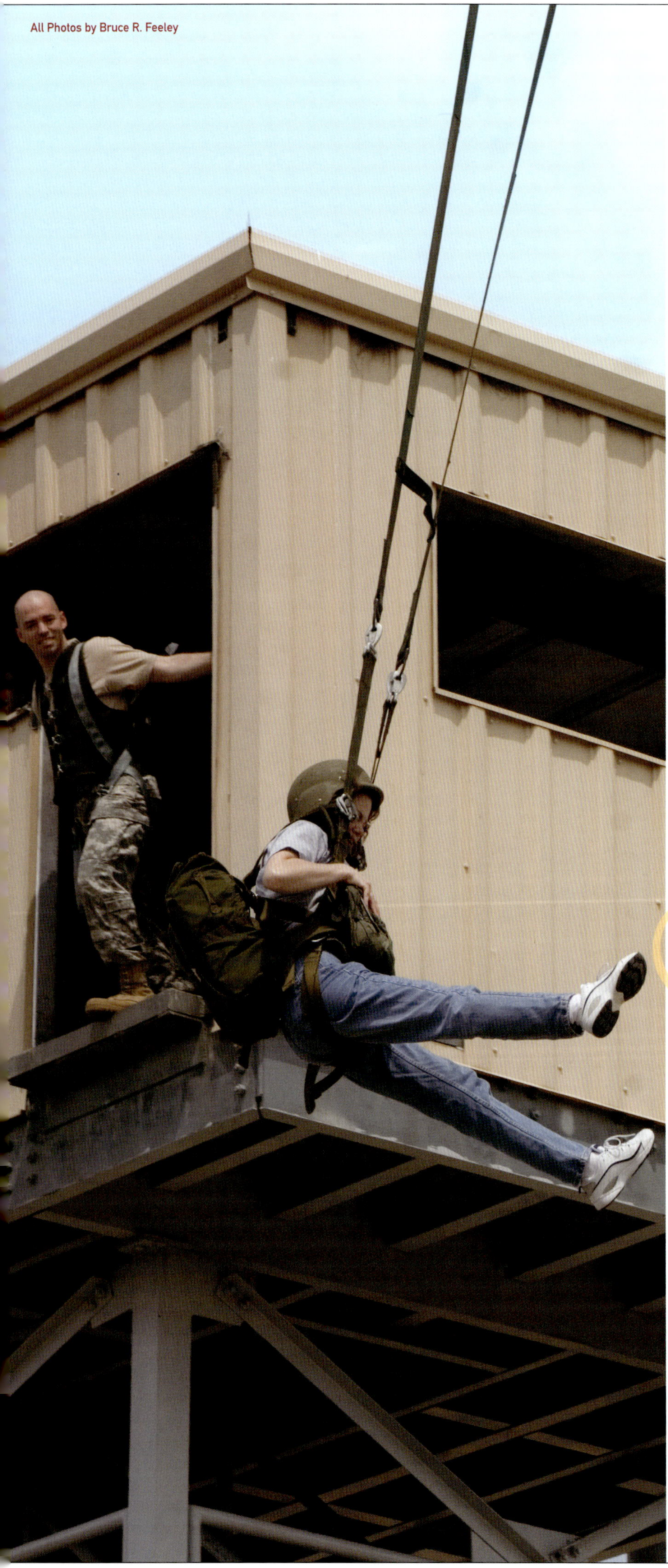

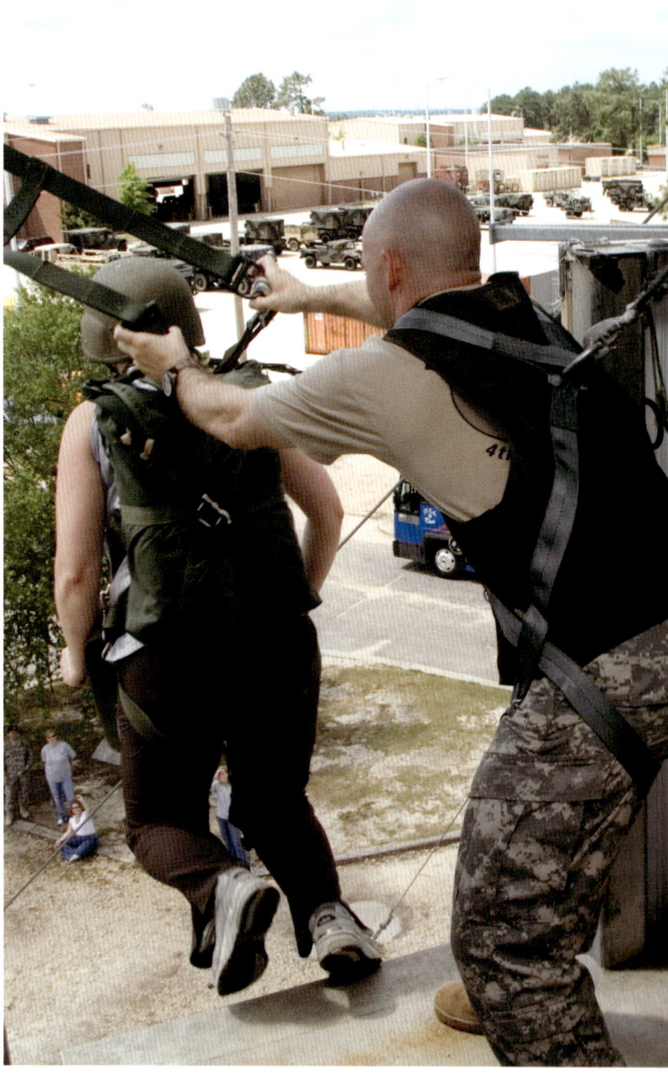

The Cumberland County Business Council's Leadership Program, which began in 1982, is still going strong. As part of the program's Military Day, members get to jump out of the Eighty-second Airborne's thirty-four-foot tower. It may look scary, but those who have tried it say it's "way cool."

Holmes Electric Security is very involved in the community. Duncan Hubbard *(right)*, central station manager with Holmes, is the current president of Fayetteville Crimestoppers.

DUPONT FAYETTEVILLE
Works to Make Science Relevant

While the average person probably isn't familiar with terms like perfluoropropyl vinyl ether, he or she doesn't have to be. All that person needs to know is the name DuPont. Founded in 1802 with explosives as its primary business, the DuPont Company has grown into a leader in several industries, delivering innovative science-based solutions that make a real difference in people's lives worldwide in areas such as food and nutrition, health care, electronics, and safety and security.

Many of those solutions are developed at DuPont Fayetteville Works. Opened in 1971 to manufacture Butacite®, a laminate for safety glass used in the automotive and architectural markets, the plant has become a key site for the DuPont Company, expanding its repertoire to include an array of pioneering products. "The products we produce improve the safety, health, and standard of living for millions of people around the globe," explains Barry Hudson, plant manager. For instance, the Nafion® and Fluoromonomer operation manufactures Nafion® film that is used in fuel cells to convert hydrogen or methanol into electricity. The SentryGlas® Plus plant produces a polymer laminate that is used for hurricane protection in the architectural market. And in late 2007, a new Tedlar® resin plant is scheduled to open for the production of a polyvinyl fluoride polymer that serves as a backing sheet in solar panels and as a protective film in the transportation industry.

Together, these divisions of Fayetteville Works have greatly boosted the local economy of Cumberland County, bringing new business opportunities to the area and creating new jobs for Fayetteville's skilled workforce. The facility boasts more than 470 employees and 350 full-time resident contractors, numbers that increase regularly as Fayetteville Works continues to be a growth site for DuPont. "Our people are our most valuable asset," Hudson notes. "Our employees reflect the diversity of race and gender in our surrounding communities, and we believe that diversity of thought provides a business advantage."

Also advantageous for DuPont is the local plant's dedication to adhering to the company's overall operating philosophy, which is rooted in its core values: safety and health, environmental stewardship, ethical behavior, and respectful treatment of people. "We will not operate any of our processes unless we are confident that we can do so without injuring our employees, our communities, or the environment," he continues.

That same commitment can also be seen in Fayetteville Works' community-oriented efforts. "As DuPonters, we believe we should give back to our community," Hudson says. Therefore, not only are many employees involved in local charities and economic development initiatives, but Fayetteville Works also contributes resources to everything from the Cumberland County Plant Managers to Habitat for Humanity. According to Hudson, the reason is simple: "The community gives us the right to operate."

He concludes, "We want to thank our customers, our employees, and the community for their support during the last thirty-six years, and we look forward to a future filled with promising opportunities." ✩

(far left)
The most recent site expansion is the new Tedlar® plant, which is shown here under construction. It opened in late 2007. Tedlar® is a polyvinyl fluoride polymer that is used as a backing sheet in solar panels and as a protective film in the transportation industry.

(below)
In July 2005, the SentryGlas® Plus plant came on line, producing polymer laminate that is used in the architectural market for hurricane glass protection. Here, a highly trained technician operates equipment used to produce this valuable product.

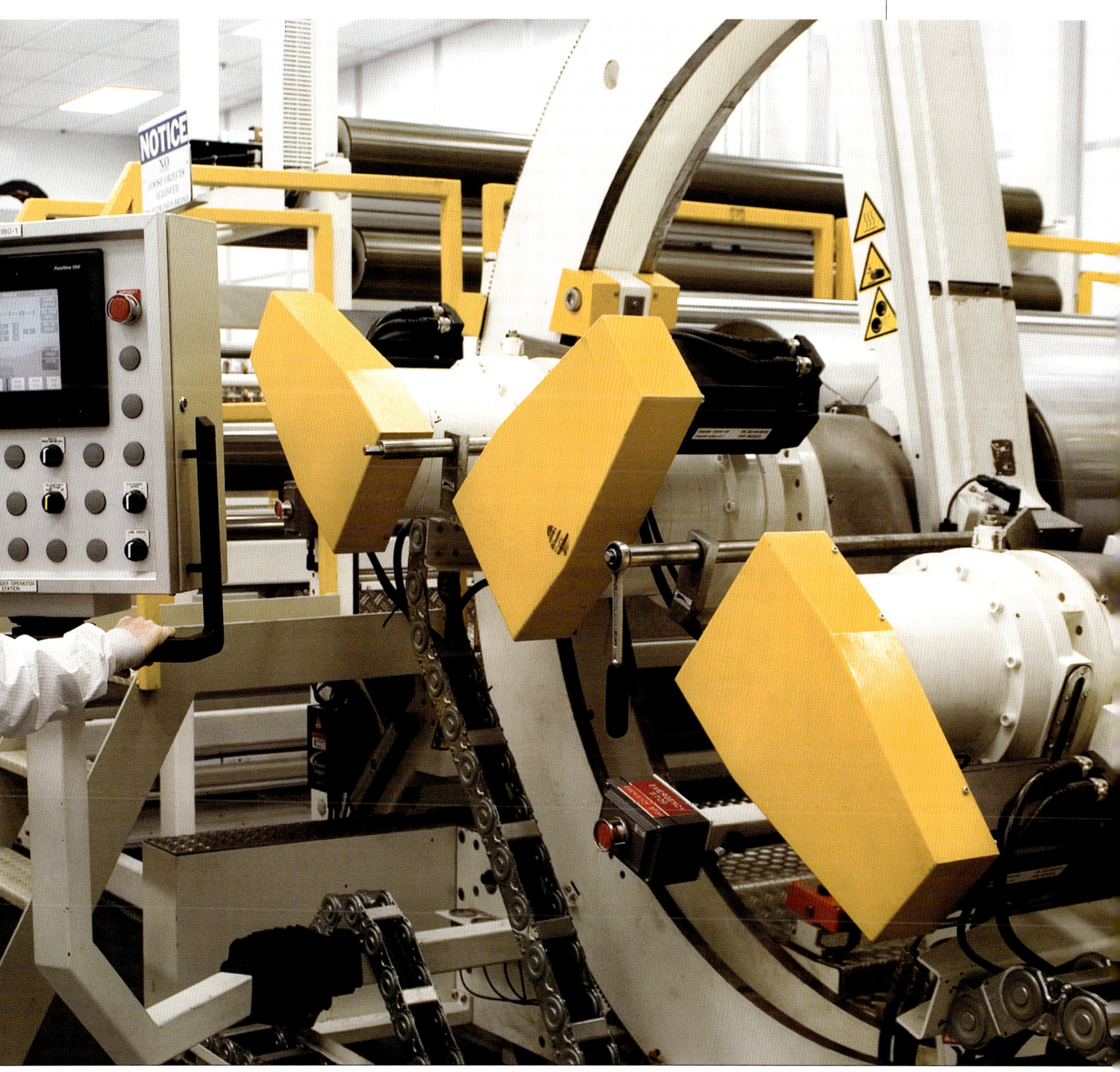

What's the secret to tossing pizza dough? "Practice. You can learn to do it in five minutes and practice doing it for twenty years," said Spero Poulos, owner of Spinners Pizza on Raeford Road. Offering takeout, buffet, or in-house dining, Spinners' specialty is New York–style pizza with the thinner crust and slightly sweet sauce that tastes better with every bite. Sub sandwiches, lasagna, and pasta are also on the menu, and customers constantly compliment the fresh salad bar. The restaurant, in business since 1999, is especially popular with families and local sports teams. Unlike chain pizza parlors, Spinners' pizza dough and sauce are homemade, but an intangible element adds the final touch. "I'm always there because I want to make sure that everything looks and tastes good," Poulos said. "How much you care makes the biggest difference, and you can't break that down into one ingredient." ★

When two guys who love beer—Dean Ogan and Kevin Summers—put their heads together, it's no surprise that they decided to open a restaurant that featured the best locally brewed beer. Thus was the Mash House Restaurant and Brewery born. The beer begins in the grain silo out front, is converted into mash with the addition of water, then ferments and ages in the custom-designed brew house. "By brewing on site and using old-world methods, no preservatives, and only the finest malted barley, hops, yeast, and pure water, we offer our customers the freshest pint possible," say the owners. Danielle Veazey adds, "Don't forget the steaks and chops that go along with the beer. Perfect by the plate, paradise by the pint, that's us." ★

Photo by Greg Foster

Photo by John Chang McCurdy

Since 1969, tires have been rolling off the line of one of the largest tire plants in the world.

GOODYEAR TIRE & RUBBER:
Developing Long-Term Financial Relationships

Here in Fayetteville, "Goodyear" means good jobs, goodwill, and hundreds of millions of dollars back into local communities.

Say the name "Goodyear," and naturally everyone thinks of tires. In Fayetteville, however, the name Goodyear means far more. As one of the largest tire manufacturing facilities in the world, the Fayetteville plant has a significant impact on the economies of Cumberland and surrounding counties. Here in Fayetteville, "Goodyear" means good jobs, goodwill, and hundreds of millions of dollars back into local communities.

In 1969, the Fayetteville plant, then operating under the name of Kelly-Springfield Tire Company (a wholly owned subsidiary of Goodyear Tire & Rubber Co.), began producing its first tires as a result of the country's expanding demand for automotive tires. The original ticket—the number of tires produced in one day—was 12,500. Today, the Fayetteville plant has become one of the largest tire plants in the world with 2.2 million square feet to handle a product mix of passenger, high-performance, and light truck tires.

As one of the area's largest employers, the Goodyear Fayetteville plant currently employs approximately twenty-six hundred associates. These same associates, and the hundreds before them, have also given their time and treasure over the years to local nonprofits, educational institutions, and the arts, including the United Way of Cumberland County, the Airborne and Special Operations Museum, Cape Fear Museum of History, Methodist University, Fayetteville State University, and Fayetteville Technical Community College.

Clearly, Goodyear's corporate presence for the past four decades is a story of commitment and a promise of continued support to help the area prosper. ★

One of fifty-nine institutions in the North Carolina Community College System, Fayetteville Technical Community College serves about thirteen thousand people in curriculum programs each year. Another twenty-eight thousand people take advantage of the technical college's continuing education programs, many of which are conducted in this building. However, understanding that learning also needs to be convenient for today's just-in-time business world, FTCC has been a pioneer in the development of alternative educational offerings. In 1981, the college offered telecourses. By 1996, FTCC was one of the first in the system to offer Internet-based courses. Each year, several thousand students take advantage of technology-enhanced curriculum either in their own home or at the workplace. ★

Photo by Bruce R. Feeley

SMITH BARNEY:
Making Your Wealth Work for You

With roots dating back to 1873, Smith Barney has become one of the world's largest and most respected financial services firms.

At Smith Barney, wealth management is more than a ubiquitous term on Wall Street; it is a way of life.

With roots dating back to 1873, Smith Barney has become one of the world's largest and most respected financial services firms. From more than six hundred offices worldwide, approximately thirteen thousand financial advisors manage in excess of $1.2 trillion in assets for some 9 million clients. In fact, with each financial advisor averaging over sixteen years experience and managing upward of $90 million in assets, Smith Barney's people are some of the most experienced in the industry.

Backed by the resources of its parent company, Citigroup Inc., Smith Barney advisors have the tools they need to service their wealth management clients. One of the world's most diversified financial services firms, with more than three hundred thousand personnel in more than one hundred countries, Citigroup is also one of the world's most profitable companies, touting an enviable record of twenty-one consecutive years of increases in shareholder dividends.

For more than fifty years, residents of Fayetteville have been receiving financial advice from Smith Barney and its predecessor firms. Founded in a downtown office in the 1950s, the Fayetteville branch is now located in One Village Plaza, in a landmark structure that many refer to as the Smith Barney Building.

From this distinctive address, Smith Barney's dedicated wealth management advisors provide high-caliber financial advice, appropriately personalized to each client. "Suitability is imperative," explains Patricia Collie, vice president of wealth management and branch manager. "We work with clients based on their individual objectives and risk parameters, and we believe in educating clients so that they can make informed decisions about their financial planning."

Smith Barney's time-tested methods look at a client's entire financial situation, working collaboratively with their existing tax and legal advisors to put together a complete strategy for investing wisely and planning for the future. "We take a holistic approach with our clients as we earn the right to be their trusted advisors," says Collie. "Our wealth management platform enables us to address both sides of our clients' balance sheets with services that range from alternative investments and managed money to comprehensive financial planning and sophisticated lending strategies." In fact, its comprehensiveness, innovation, and individualized attention earned Smith Barney a top honor as High Net-Worth

Leader of the Year 2006 by Private Asset Management, a subsidiary of Institutional Investor.*

Smith Barney strategies also address issues that impact future generations. "The topic of finance is intimidating to many people who, oftentimes, put it on the back burner," says Collie. "But once life gets so complicated, it is really important to seek professional advice to evaluate your financial situation, and we can help clients address their wealth transfer issues as well as lifestyle and family advisory issues."

Indeed, family and community are so important to Smith Barney that the firm gives back through both dollars and volunteer hours. "We have a tremendously strong commitment to the community because we are the

(Continued on page 152)

All Photos by Bruce R. Feeley

Photo by Bruce R. Feeley

Photo by Bruce R. Feeley

(Smith Barney continued from page 151)

community," says Collie. "We actually participate in the community by serving on local boards of nonprofits and as volunteers for various nonprofit and civic organizations."

Of particular charitable interest to the Fayetteville branch are support of the Academy of Finance at Douglas Byrd High School, a preparedness program for students interested in the field of finance, and of the Child Advocacy Center, which works with abused and neglected children. Financial advisor Tommy Bolton, who serves in an honorary capacity as civilian aide to the secretary of the army for North Carolina, is an example of Smith Barney employees' other commitment, supporting our soldiers and their families. Participation in activities like these, the firm knows, can help everyone have a better quality of life. ✶

The devotion between the Fayetteville Police Department's K9 Unit officers and their dogs is mutual as they spend long hours training and working together. The dogs, purchased in Holland, are Belgian Malinois, a high-energy breed known for agility, obedience, and intelligence. These characteristics make them suitable for such activities as narcotics detection, rescue and search, tracking, and other police work. Here Sergeant Tracey Campbell completes an apprehension exercise with his canine friend. The dogs begin training as puppies and can remain on the force for ten years or more, depending on their health. They work well with multiple handlers and have been recognized along with their human partners for meritorious service. Upon retirement, their loyalty and hard work is returned: they are frequently adopted by their handlers. ✺

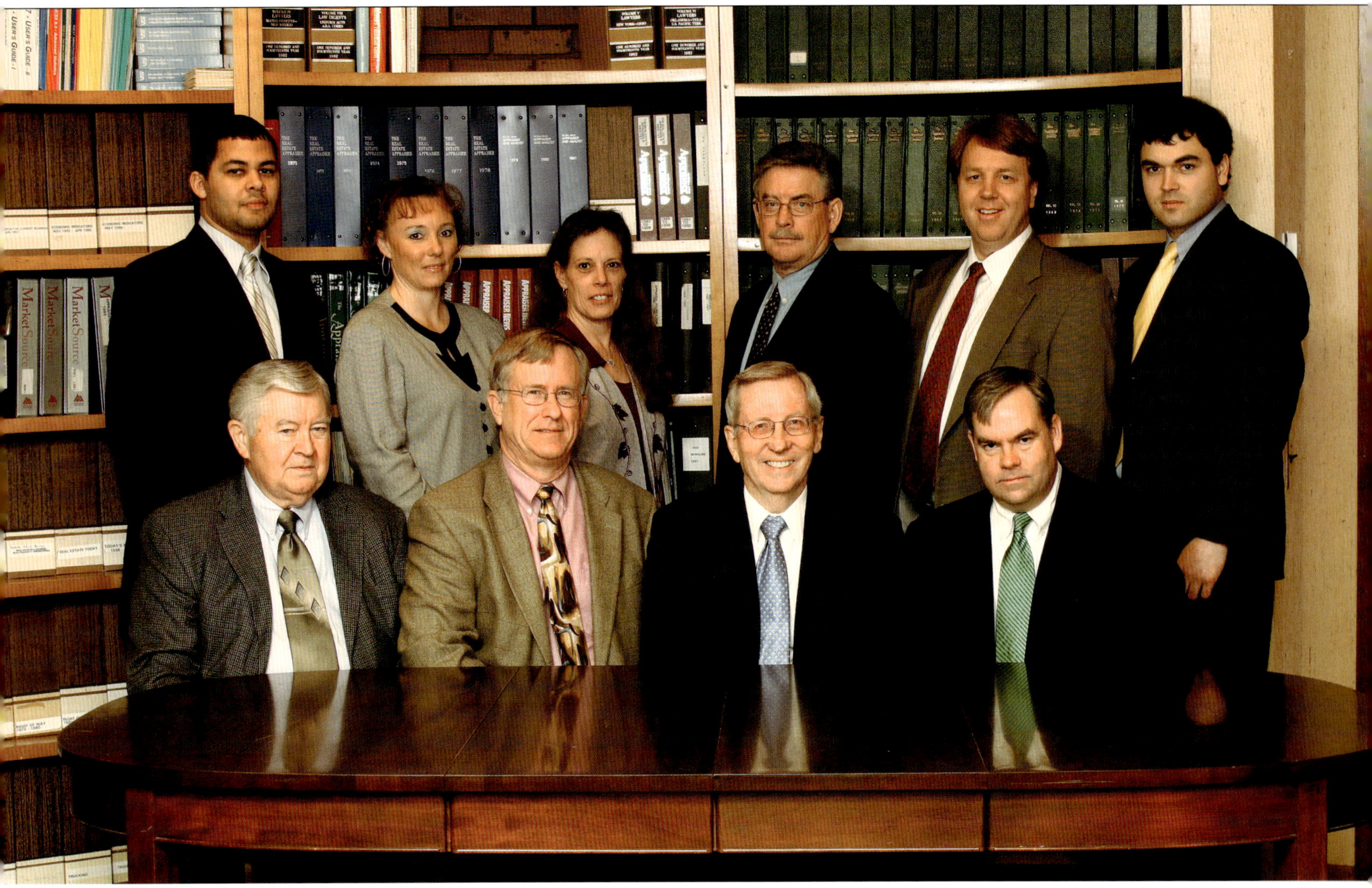

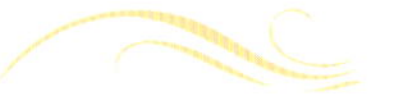

Photo by John Chang McCurdy

The team of professionals at Tom Keith & Associates Inc. bring to the table a broad base of experience, a thorough understanding of the region's business and real estate market, and knowledge of the importance of objective, accurate valuations. (Front row, left to right) *R. Cecil Carlyle, John German, Tom Keith, and Thomas Bell;* (back row, left to right) *Aaron Locklear, Kelly Williams, Paula Mitchell, James Bullard, David Duke, and J. Carr Gibson.*

TOM KEITH & ASSOCIATES:

Valuation Performance Counts

"We understand the risks as well as the benefits and advise our clients accordingly."

As a youngster, Fayetteville area native Tom Keith remembers much of his family's dinner table talk focusing on real estate and business. "My family has owned property in southeastern NC since 1832," he says, "so I was exposed to valuable real estate and business knowledge from a very young age."

It's no surprise that after graduating from college and working for several years in the family business, Keith started his own real estate, business, and consulting firm. Established in 1970, Tom Keith & Associates has provided valuation and consulting services for over three-thousand clients, including Fortune 500 companies, private firms, government entities, manufacturers, and individual buyers, sellers, and investors.

Holding certifications in both business valuation and commercial real estate appraisal, the company's team of specialists provides services for sale, purchase, and lease transactions, as well as for loan, gift, and estate tax valuations, damage suits, shareholder disputes, tax appeals, and absorption rate and feasibility studies. Tom Keith & Associates is also qualified to allocate the value of both tangible and intangible assets as well as the total enterprise.

"Since we've been doing this for over thirty-seven years, we've experienced many recessions and expansions," says Keith. "We understand the risks as well as the benefits and advise our clients accordingly. Our objective is to put our clients on the right path at the right time for maximum benefit."

"I'm proud of our team because they have proven that they will meet the demands placed before them, and I would challenge any practitioner to match our experience and performance."

Situated at the intersection of Green, Gillespie, Person, and Hay streets, Fayetteville's Market House was built in 1832 as the city's center for commerce and government. It has remained a center for public life in Fayetteville ever since. For decades, local farmers sold their meat and produce beneath the arches while the second floor served as the town hall. In recent years the second floor has been used as a public library, chamber of commerce offices, and an art museum. Listed on the National Register of Historic Places, the building's unique architecture mimics nineteenth-century English town hall/market designs. Even the clock is still in use, chiming at 7:30 a.m. for breakfast, 1:00 p.m. for dinner, at sundown, and at 9:00 p.m., to mark the traditional curfew hour. ★

Photo by Alan S. Weiner

With every customer, Carolina Mortgage Company earns its reputation as a locally owned business that completes loans in a fast and friendly manner. The staff strives to consistently provide convenient and quality service, and as a result Carolina Mortgage is one of the largest VA lenders in North Carolina. Here Diann Peters, closing secretary, assists Mr. and Mrs. Olvera with the completion of a mortgage application.

CAROLINA MORTGAGE COMPANY:
Local and Loyal Lenders

"We have the best turnaround time in the industry."

The people at Carolina Mortgage Company in Fayetteville, North Carolina, know how stressful applying for a home mortgage can be, so they have made it their mission to combat the impersonal service that is often typical of larger lending institutions. With three offices in the Fayetteville/Fort Bragg/Pope AFB region, Carolina Mortgage is one of the largest VA lenders in the state, and a VA Automatic Lender. Being owned and operated locally allows this mortgage company to complete all work onsite, giving clients the personal care and expedited service that they deserve. "We have the best turnaround time in the industry," says Dave Allred, president.

Founded in 1986, this mortgage company's years of success have precipitated the opening of a sister company, Atlantic First Mortgage Corporation, with offices in Jacksonville and Asheville, North Carolina. Using convenient online application forms, customers can determine the mortgage amount they qualify for within twenty-four hours (even before house hunting begins), and funding is typically available within days instead of weeks. Prequalification and preapproval programs include a lock-and-shop program for locking in current interest rates while customers shop for a home. Offering a full range of conventional, FHA, and VA loans—all tailored to each customer's individual needs, and delivered with hands-on care and expertise—the staff at Carolina Mortgage Company accomplishes its mission one satisfied customer at a time. ★

For the best hand-cut steaks, fall-off-the-bone ribs, and made-from-scratch side orders around, head over to the Texas Roadhouse, a place where memories are made. "Our mission is 'Legendary Food and Legendary Service,'" says proprietor Mark Hymes, "and what that means is it's something that people are going to remember and talk about for a long time." In addition to mouthwatering menu items, ice-cold beer, and a bounty of specialty margaritas, diners are treated to an hourly line-dance show by a bevy of high-spirited servers. ✩

Photo by Bruce R. Feeley

Photo by Alan S. Weiner

HODGES ASSOCIATES:
Creative "Products" Create Results

When it comes to creativity, the agency's president, Anna Hodges Smith, says, "It's the 'product' we provide for our clients."

If you . . .

. . . get a press release from FYI Fayetteville, the area's "news bureau."

. . . have been "greeted" in a welding store by the image of Richard Petty or Monster Garage host Jesse James.

. . . search for government contract opportunities, job candidates, or employment on MatchForce.com.

. . . are enticed by an I-95 billboard to Stop and Smell the Flowers at Cape Fear Botanical Garden.

. . . are checked out in the supermarket by someone wearing a button that says Got id? No? Get milk!

. . . had your interest in a retractable awning piqued by a flyer saying Make a Statement. And Retract It.

. . . get information from the City of Fayetteville's Waste Management Department telling you they're At Your Disposal.

. . . buy a home in Anderson Creek Club, a gated, golf-course community Where Luxury Begins and the Vacation Never Ends.

. . . are a CEO who was invited to explore the benefits of locating your business in Fayetteville during a weekend of History, Heroes and 18 Hallowed Holes.

. . . have been encouraged to conserve electricity and water by Guy Wire, the super-sleuth spokesman for Fayetteville's Public Works Commission (PWC)—

Then you are also familiar with some of the creative work of Hodges Associates!

Established in Fayetteville in 1974, Hodges Associates is a full-service marketing, advertising, and public relations agency. Over the past four decades, the Fayetteville-based agency has been putting its marketing expertise and creative talents to work for a growing number of clients. While most of Hodges's clients are based in the southeastern region, several are national or international in scope. They include one of the world's largest producers of welding and cutting products and one of the nation's leading producers and distributors of industrial fabrics.

When it comes to creativity, the agency's president, Anna Hodges Smith, says, "It's the 'product' we provide for our clients." But, as Smith explains, creativity is more than memorable, attention-grabbing words and compelling design. It's the ability to visualize, develop, and implement unique marketing, branding, and communications strategies that will achieve success for every client and every project.

Hodges Associates has also been a strong advocate for its home community. The agency has provided extensive marketing support—on both a business and pro bono basis—for greater Fayetteville itself, as well as for area events, attractions, institutions, and projects for the greater good.

Whether they're helping their community prosper—or helping clients raise awareness, increase sales, and capture new market share—Hodges Associates is in the "business" of creating . . . creating notable results. ★

Train buffs are familiar with the Palmetto and the Silver Service Amtrak trains which operate north-south between New York City and Miami. Fayetteeville is one of the many stations served along the 1,389-mile route. The Palmetto offers business class service, including complimentary non-alcoholic beverages, newspapers, audio entertainment, priority boarding, and other amenities. Silver Meteor trains include Viewliner sleeping and dining car accommodations. Connecting trains also serve Boston, Chicago, New Orleans, and Los Angeles. Amtrak has two daily trains out of Fayetteville. ✶

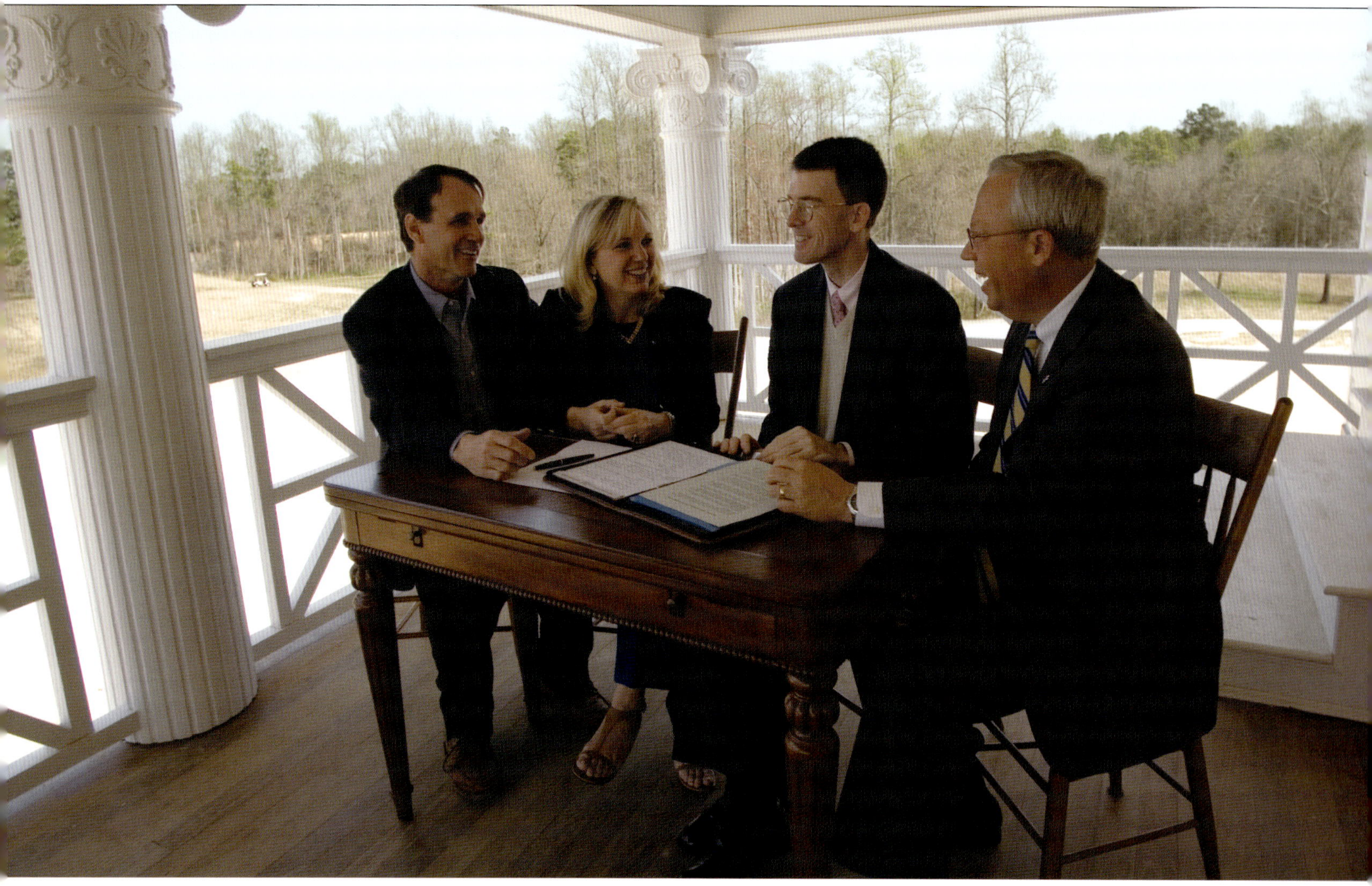

Photo by Rod Reilly

On the porch of their historic home, Max and Sue Faykus (left) discuss details of the building's move and restoration with First Citizens account officer Stuart Walters and Cumberland-area executive Tim Richardson. The Faykuses are personal and business customers of First Citizens, which specializes in helping its customers achieve a lifetime of success.

FIRST CITIZENS BANK:
Valuing Long-Term Financial Relationships

"Our goals are to provide life-enhancing financial services and to be the bank of choice in the community."

First Citizens Bank's ties to Fayetteville go back to 1934 when the North Carolina–headquartered company opened its first office in the community. Five years later, First Citizens became one of the first commercial banks in the nation to operate on a military base when it opened a branch at nearby Fort Bragg.

Today, First Citizens continues as a vital presence in Cumberland County, serving the needs of individuals and businesses in the Fayetteville area as well as military personnel and their families at Fort Bragg and the adjacent Pope Air Force Base.

Long-term, satisfied customers are a hallmark of this bank, which was founded in Smithfield, North Carolina, in 1898. First Citizens now operates 340 branches in five states with thirteen offices in Cumberland County, all operating with the original values of integrity, common sense, and trust-building consistency.

Perhaps the personal touch that First Citizens' customers feel stems from the bank's North Carolina roots and the fact that it is one of the largest family-controlled banks in the United States. The bank specializes in meeting the financial needs of individuals, small- to mid-size businesses, medical practices, and other professionals.

"Our goals are to provide life-enhancing financial services and to be the bank of choice in the community," says Tim Richardson, the bank's Cumberland-area executive. "We do that by delving deep into our financial relationships with our customers so we can identify and provide the services they need. Our team remains devoted to making solid and exceptional client relationships a reality." ★

The tallest building in downtown Fayetteville, North Carolina, Systel's office complex is considered the city's premier business address. Systel is the Southeast's largest independent dealer of office automation equipment and a multiple recipient of the Dealer Award presented by *Office Dealer* magazine. With nine locations across North Carolina and Georgia, Systel chose beautiful Fayetteville as the seat of its corporate offices. A revitalization effort over the past few years has quickly made the city an ever-more popular location for commerce, arts, shopping, and dining. Building tenants in the Systel building have a view of the Cross Creek Linear Park Fountain across the street on Ray Avenue, a perfect spot to have a bite to eat during lunch hour.

Photo by Bruce R. Feeley

Photo by Rod Reilly

Jerry Gregory (left), president of Jerry Gregory & Associates, discusses coverages with Stephen Wheeler, president of Holmes Electric Security Systems. Like many customers, Wheeler is a long-term client of JG&A's, having done business together for over fifteen years.

JERRY GREGORY & ASSOCIATES:
Our Business Is Insurance; Our Customers Are Family

"We're not about pushing products, but about knowing our clients and bringing solutions to the table."

How does a retired captain of the USAF Reserves become the president of his own insurance brokerage agency? Jerry Gregory did so by learning the business from the ground up while retaining a true concern for people. Gregory completed college and worked his way through the insurance industry in a variety of career capacities that currently serve him well as the top executive of Jerry Gregory & Associates. Based in Fayetteville, North Carolina, JG&A specializes in matching small and large businesses with the right fit of employee group health benefits, dental, life, disability, Health Reimbursement Accounts, and Health Savings Accounts..

JG&A serves over 160 group clients, representing over $55 million in annualized premiums and is regularly recognized as one of the top producers in the United States. "Our philosophy is 'We take care of people,'" said Gregory. "We're not about pushing products, but about knowing our clients and bringing solutions to the table." This successful approach, combined with an in-depth knowledge of the insurance business, earns the company long-term clients and a reputation for treating customers as friends, not commodities, in a highly competitive industry.

JG&A supports numerous charities, including regular contributions to a local free medical clinic for those without health insurance, and Gregory served on the board of the United Way for six years. "We have loyalty to our clients and to our community, and in return, they have a lot of loyalty to us," he said. ✹

The Cumberland County Board of Commissioners is a seven-member entity, five of whom are elected from one of two districts in the county and two who are elected at-large. Cumberland County operates with a board of commissioners/county manager form of government. Each commissioner is elected for a four-year term. The terms are staggered, and the members elect their own chairman and vice-chairman annually. The board of commissioners meets twice monthly, the first Monday of the month at 9 a.m. and the third Monday at 6:45 p.m., in the County Commissioners Meeting Room (Room 118) of the Cumberland County Court House. The meetings are televised live on Time Warner Cable Channel 7. Agendas for the meetings are posted on the county's Web site, www.co.cumberland.nc.us. ★

Photo by Bruce R. Feeley

The Register of Deeds office, located on the first floor of the Cumberland County Court House, touches every citizen's life sooner or later. It is here that one can obtain birth certificates, death certificates, military discharge papers (DD214s), and marriage licenses; it's also where the deeds to property in the county are recorded. Land records date back to 1754, when Cumberland County was officially established. In the photo above, Westley Whitmore and Shacuara Hunter are applying for a marriage license and proudly showing assistant register of deeds Diana Fisher and deputy register of deeds Barbara Watts (*right*) the wedding rings. Register of deeds is an elected position, currently held by Lee Warren. ★

The mounted patrol unit is a vital element of many municipal police departments. The City of Fayetteville's unit began in 1998, funded in part by the Downtown Business Alliance. Serving a primary purpose of monitoring heavily populated areas such as shopping and entertainment districts, the unit is not just for show. It enforces traffic by running hand-held radar, patrols parking areas to prevent break-ins, and finds missing children in crowds. As such, the horses are well-prepared for their work. These steeds are well-mannered and courteous, and they remain calm under conditions that might excite other horses. Each horse in the City of Fayetteville's mounted patrol unit is carefully trained, with exposure to a variety of noises they will encounter on the job, including horns, sirens, traffic sounds, and the most problematic of all: garbage trucks. Because their beauty and status draw the interest of children and adults, they must also be gentle enough to allow for a friendly pat or a treat. Their magnetism brings another benefit to the police department. People will go out of their way to meet the officer and his horse, and will then begin a conversation that will impart key information. ★

ERA PENNINK & STROTHER REAL ESTATE:
Where Everyone is Family

"Success begets success, so it was only natural that successful agents wanted to join our company."

In the same way the family is the cornerstone of civilization, the family atmosphere at ERA Pennink & Strother Real Estate is the cornerstone of their success. In 1999, the company was formed by the merger of two small real estate firms owned by Suzanne Pennink and Larry Strother.

"Two years later they purchased an ERA franchise, and things really took off," said Greg West, general manager. "Success begets success, so it was only natural that successful agents wanted to join our company. Now we have more than fifty full-time agents, we've moved into new offices, and we're one of the top companies in the residential real estate market."

Obviously, this is an extremely hard-working group, but the owners know the importance of allotting time for fellowship, for quarterly covered-dish birthday celebrations, and for having fun with costumes at Halloween and door-decorating contests at Christmas. This sense of community and caring carries over into their day-to-day interaction with their clients. Part of their motto states, "We believe in treating every customer like family."

Because of its proximity to Fort Bragg, the firm has an especially close relationship with troops stationed there. "We provide special training for our brokers who work with the military," said West. A number of the staff are retired military who bring firsthand experience to their jobs.

A good example of the customer service Pennink & Strother provides can be seen in a letter from a soldier written to agent Ben Cheney. "I have been in Iraq for almost three months, and my wife has asked for your assistance on many occasions. I can't thank you enough."

Another kind of recognition was given to agent Masha Cooke, who was one of the top ten finalists—from among thirty-eight thousand ERA agents nationwide—for the Jim Jackson Memorial Award for customer service. This award, named for the late founder and president of ERA, is voted on by consumers.

This kind of personalized service to all clients has helped the firm build its reputation not only in Fayetteville but on a national basis. ERA Pennink & Strother was named as a Gene Francis Award Finalist, an honor given to only the top five companies in the entire ERA system.

The ERA story is also an impressive one. From its beginning more than thirty years ago, ERA has stayed on the cutting edge of technology. In fact, ERA stands for Electronic Realty Associates. The company pioneered the use of fax machines in every office, and they were the first real estate company to post all their listings online. ERA continued to be an innovator by launching its own Web site in 1995.

ERA Pennink & Strother seems to have found the perfect balance of cutting-edge technology and family values, a combination that produces outstanding service to all its clients. ✸

(far left)

From exciting condominiums and townhouses to single-family homes, ERA Pennink & Strother Real Estate sells more new construction than any other company in Fayetteville. No detail is too small to make their customers' dreams come true.

(below)

ERA Pennink & Strother agents are leaders in the marketing and sales of existing homes in the greater Fayetteville area. The firm takes pride in being on the front lines promoting all that is great about Fayetteville.

All Photos by Alan S. Weiner

The Holiday Inn Bordeaux suits the needs of all types of travelers. Business people enjoy keeping connected with high-speed Internet access. Leisure travelers like the hotel's convenient location to Fayetteville's shopping, dining, and area attractions. Military personnel who require extended housing always feel at home here. And, as the largest hotel in the area, it's the go-to place for meetings and conventions. ✶

Designed as his first signature course in North Carolina by PGA Championship winner Davis Love III, Anderson Creek reveals everything that's great about golfing in the Carolina Sandhills. Love took full advantage of the natural terrain to create rolling fairways lined with mature longleaf pines and strategically placed love grass mixed with natural grass and sand in the rough areas. The result is a first-class golfing experience, reflected in such accolades as Best New Course in North Carolina for 2001 and a Five Star rating for 2002. The eighteen-hole course is situated within Anderson Creek Club, a private gated community nestled among seventeen hundred acres of rolling pine forest.

Photo by Alan S. Weiner

RE/MAX CHOICE:
Hometown Experts with a World of Experience

Judy and Rusty Russell, along with their dogs, Job and Maddie, are pictured in front of their home in Fayetteville, North Carolina. Both are committed professionals with RE/MAX Choice, a leading real estate organization both locally and nationally. As members of the National Association of Realtors, the Russells took an oath to maintain the highest of standards, including integrity, fair dealing, and honesty. Judy and Rusty have both led the Fayetteville Association of Realtors as president..

"We offer superior service, a highly trained staff, two convenient locations, and in-depth knowledge of this market."

Judy and Rusty Russell were competitors when they met at a Christmas party at the Airborne & Special Operations Museum. Rusty was smitten from the start. When he finally built up the nerve to call Judy, he asked if she was spoken for, giving her the impression that he was a gentleman from the dark ages. They wed in 2004 and have happily ever after run RE/MAX Choice's two Fayetteville, North Carolina, offices. "You might say that we're married to each other, to our business, and to our community," says Rusty.

The two share years as real estate partners, and life experiences that serve them well as REALTORS® for the four-county region. Both were born in Germany as military brats, so they fully understand the stresses of re-locating, especially for the families of nearby Fort Bragg and Pope AFB. Both have lifelong roots in Fayetteville, where they raised their children, built a business, and support their church, the local arts, and charities such as the Fisher House, a residence for the visiting relatives of injured soldiers. Their commitment to God further upholds the high ethical standards of the National Association of Realtors, for which they have each served as local association president. "We've received a lot from this community, and we want to give back," says Judy. "We offer superior service, a highly trained staff, two convenient locations, and in-depth knowledge of this market." Rusty and Judy view their shared professional expertise and their love for Fayetteville as a good match. ✶

Serving the community since 1791, the Fayetteville Fire Department operates out of seventeen stations city-wide. The newest of these, Station 14, is located adjacent to the Fayetteville State University campus and offers fire science programs for area students. The department also provides the city with special services such as emergency medical, hazardous materials response, collapse search and rescue, and help for aircraft emergencies. In addition to answering fire and emergency calls, the department takes a proactive approach to prevention through education programs targeted at residents and businesses. ★

Photo by Rod Reilly

COHEN & GREEN SALVAGE COMPANY:
Recycling Pioneers

From something old comes something new. It's not magic. It takes hard work, years of experience, and good business sense.

In 1946, John Green and Harold Cohen started Cohen & Green Salvage Co. Inc., and the company is currently owned by Michael Green and Jerry Parsek. "When John and Harold started the business, they had a truck, a wrecker, and a torch," said Green. Today, giant cranes, forklifts, loaders, balers, trucks, trailers, and a one-thousand-ton shear handle the heavy work.

Before the recyclable materials can be processed, they have to be sorted by metal type (aluminum, copper, brass, iron, steel, etc.) and also separated into grades of the different materials. All paper, plastic, trash, and attachments must be removed.

Cohen & Green provides container and trailer services for industrial and commercial customers to handle production scrap, obsolete machinery, maintenance scrap, and other metal materials. They also have multiple car crushers that process scrap cars both at their facility and at customers' sites. Cohen & Green purchases scrap from customers who bring materials to their facility for recycling. Their mission is to purchase and process materials in a fair, safe, and environmentally responsible way, following all local, state, and federal laws and regulations. Management and employees strive to meet these goals every day.

By recycling thousands of tons of materials that would otherwise be discarded, Cohen & Green Salvage does its part to make the Fayetteville area a cleaner and healthier place to live. ✸

> "When John
> and Harold
> started the business,
> they had a truck,
> a wrecker,
> and a torch."

Fayetteville was the nation's first city to be named after the French nobleman, congressionally appointed military officer, and key supporter of the American Revolution, Marie Joseph Paul Yves Roche Gilbert du Motier, known as the Marquis de Lafayette. In 1825, after he had played a pivotal role in the Revolution, serving under the command of General George Washington, Lafayette visited his namesake city on a tour of the country. Today, a statue near the city's center honors the distinguished Frenchman. ✶

RLM COMMUNICATIONS:
Providing Total Communications System Solutions

When government and military operations need communications services, RLM Communications fills the demand with rapid, secure solutions—whether on land, on sea, or in the air.

RLM Communications, Inc. answers the call with communications solutions and staffing for all land, sea, and air operations.

The challenges of today's government and military operations demand rapid, responsive, efficient, and secure contractor services. In the realm of communications services, RLM Communications, Inc. answers the call with communications solutions and staffing for all land, sea, and air operations.

RLM Communications, Inc. was started in 2004 by Randy Lee Moore, a service-disabled veteran with more than twenty years of communications systems experience in both the public and private sectors. From design and development through operation and integration, Moore has delved into, and dealt with, the intricacies of both voice and data systems of virtually every size and scope to meet the demands of a bourgeoning communications marketplace.

Under Moore's leadership, which combines expertise with an emphasis on customer satisfaction, RLM Communications, Inc. has grown from a four-person operation into a global enterprise operating across the United States and abroad. Together, the RLM team delivers a complete list of services, including network engineering and installation, platform support and systems integration, program and project management, on-site personnel staffing and training, systems design, and advanced technology research.

In addition to its certification as a Small Disadvantaged Business, RLM Communications, Inc. participates in the Small Business Administration's 8(a) Business Development Program, a designation that gives clients an avenue for fulfilling specified government contracting requirements.

As a government contracting business entity, RLM Communications, Inc. possesses the ability to respond rapidly to emerging industry changes—a nimbleness that translates into measurable cost reductions and greater effectiveness for clients. ✶

Located in southwestern Cumberland County, Hope Mills is one of the fastest-growing towns in North Carolina. Anyone interested in the area is invited to attend the town meetings held here at the Town Hall every first and third Monday of the month. The town history dates back to 1766. Because of natural water power and an abundance of timber, a lumber camp, sawmill, gristmill, and pottery business were established. Initially the area was known as Little Rockfish Village, but after the construction of the first cotton mill in 1839 the name was changed. Unfortunately the mill and many other buildings were burned by General Sherman and his troops during the Civil War. ✶

Photo by Rod Reilly

All Photos by Alan S. Weiner

Play

The quality of life in Fayetteville and Cumberland County is enhanced significantly by the multitude of leisure activities that are available in the area. Some of the recreational offerings are furnished by Mother Nature herself, while others are products of thoughtful planning and implementation by attentive leaders and dedicated citizens. From the Great Outdoors to the Great White Way, there truly is a pastime and a venue for everyone who wants to relax and have some fun in Fayetteville and its surrounding neighborhoods.

There's no better place for alfresco activities than Fayetteville. With moderate temperatures making appearances throughout three of the four seasons and the Cape Fear River situated only moments away from many locales, fishing, canoeing, kayaking, and a host of other water sports are practically year-round diversions for residents and visitors alike. The climate also makes golfing a particularly pleasant pursuit, especially with courses like Anderson Creek and Gates Four Golf & Country Club offering some of the best tee boxes and greens around. Furthermore, the county is home to numerous community parks and recreation facilities, where everything from camping and hiking to youth and adult sports make getting exercise and getting involved easy for people of all ages. Even Fort Bragg supports its troops and their families with outdoor entertainment, including golf, tennis, swimming, equestrian activities, and much more.

Exercising the mind and the soul is equally important in Fayetteville and Cumberland County, which is why the cultural arts have become such a predominant feature in the area. For example, while Broadway hits come alive on the stage at Cape Fear Regional Theatre, the Fayetteville Symphony Orchestra makes beautiful music during its highly anticipated season each year. The local museums poignantly celebrate Cumberland County and its rich heritage, paying tribute to its military history at such locations as the National Airborne & Special Operations Museum and showing appreciation for the visual arts at venues like the Fayetteville Museum of Art and the myriad art galleries found in the area's historic districts. What's more, with the many festivals and special events that take place in the city annually, there's always a reason for residents and tourists to come out and play.

All that, along with everything else this exciting North Carolina destination has to offer, makes every day feel like a holiday in Fayetteville and Cumberland County. ✶

Dancing in the streets to multicultural music in a color-filled Parade of Nations is only a portion of the excitement that attracts seventy thousand visitors a year to Fayetteville's two-day International Folk Festival. For almost three decades, representatives of thirty countries have convened to celebrate their native heritage and share their love of America. Based on a platform of performance and visual arts, this gathering offers arts and crafts, the opportunity to sample indigenous recipes at the International Café, music, games, and more. The Arts Council of Fayetteville/Cumberland County presents this event, which the Southeast Tourism Society has named one of the Top 20 Festivals in the Southeast. A different host country is featured every year, allowing visitors to learn more about the global neighbors of the United States, or maybe their neighbor next door. ✺

GERMANY
FRENCH
FRIES
les étu
de fra
Mass
Classical H
High School
High Schoo

CROWN CENTER:
An Entertainment Hub
Making Great Memories

Five great venues comprise the Crown Center, providing accommodations for gatherings of every size and purpose.

Whether it's an annual convention, sold-out concert, or intimate wedding celebration, the Crown Center is a place where memories are made. "We are always working on ways to create a positive memory for people because our vision is to be the hub of entertainment for southeastern North Carolina," explains Rick Reno, chief executive officer.

Five great venues comprise the Crown Center, providing accommodations for gatherings of every size and purpose.

As the jewel of the complex, the Crown Coliseum has been a place of excitement since 1997, hosting everything from world-class stage acts to monster truck rallies to high school graduations. Convertible to an ice rink or sports field, the coliseum is also home to the Southern Professional Hockey League's Fayetteville FireAntz and the National Indoor Football League's Fayetteville Guard.

The Crown Exposition Center has provided attendees with plenty of space for wheeling and dealing since its opening in 1987. With 1.3 acres of space, readily divisible into smaller sections of eighty-nine hundred to sixty thousand square feet, this part of the complex is ideal for meetings as well as commercial exhibits promoting everything from flower gardens to firearm collections.

As the site of rodeos and wrestling matches, circuses and concerts, the Crown Arena has long been a place of whooping and hollering. One of the original complex structures, built in 1967, the renovated arena can seat up to five thousand or hold a stage up to twenty-four hundred square feet. The acoustically superb twenty-four-hundred-seat Crown Theatre, another original structure, has always been a showcase for plays and ballets, orchestras and orators. And the complex ballroom and hospitality area, situated between the coliseum and exposition center, is perfect for more intimate gatherings of six hundred or fewer guests.

Whichever location is best suited, Crown Center expertise can create an event to be remembered. For instance, when Queen Noor of Jordan visited for the Fayetteville Symphony's fiftieth anniversary celebration, the Crown transformed its arena into a reception area befitting royalty. By the same token, each year the Cumberland County Fair takes over every inch of the Crown complex.

Beyond space, Crown Center amenities encompass catering, concessions, production, event management, marketing, sales, and more. Even special requests are no problem for the Crown Center staff and can include specially prepared meals and décor to meet the exact specifications of the most discriminating clients.

Whatever amenities an event dictates, every client can look forward to one kind of service: "First class," says Reno. "We can handle the entire event, and we can do it at the level that you expect."

Over the course of a decade, events have brought more than 6.5 million people to the Crown Center. Fulfilling their expectations is a crew of professionals certified in all aspects of facility operations whose varied knowledge keeps the complex at the industry's leading edge. "The face of our staff is one of diversity," says Reno. "We have people from different cultures,

(Continued on page 184)

(far left)

The versatile Crown Exposition Center transforms to host many types of events, including the Cumberland County Fair, trade shows, and banquets of all sizes.

(below)

When it comes to entertainment, the Crown Coliseum is the place to be in Fayetteville. Opened in 1997, the Crown Coliseum is the site of world-class concerts, performances, and ice shows, as well as minor league hockey. Capable of seating more than eleven thousand, the coliseum is also a premier gathering place for community events like graduations and conventions.

(Crown Center continued from page 183)

different backgrounds, and different experiences. And we always try to infuse our staff with younger people who help keep us up to date on the acts that are selling now, on who's the next big thing."

Together, these professionals build team spirit by practicing what they call "CPR," or treating each other with courtesy, professionalism, and respect. "As long as we apply CPR to any issue we may have, we can resolve it," explains Reno.

That same treatment extends to clients as well and, when combined with the philosophy to "do right, do it right, do it right now," results in positive outcomes for clientele, no matter how hectic things can get. "We can't go wrong as long as we're doing the right thing, doing it

(above)

The Crown Theatre's newly renovated atrium lobby serves as the entryway into a unique cultural atmosphere. Inside the theatre, patrons experience all forms of art, from dance and music to national touring Broadway productions.

(left)

Held each September, the Cumberland County Fair is a traditional agricultural fair that showcases livestock displays and auctions. Dozens of carnival rides and vendors line the midway to provide family fun to more than sixty thousand visitors. The fair takes place at the Crown Center, filling every corner of the complex with a variety of entertainment for all ages.

to the best of our abilities, and remembering that time is of the essence in this business," says Reno.

It's a formula that is continuing to bring the Crown Center success in a constantly evolving industry. In fact, in celebration of its tenure, the Crown Center held a monthlong celebration in October 2007, marking the fortieth anniversary of the opening of its arena and theatre, twentieth anniversary of the exposition center, and the tenth anniversary of the coliseum. It was a memorable occasion for a complex that is continually finding ways to give clients some of the best memories of their lives. ✯

(above)

Patrons pack the house at the Crown Arena as professional bullriders compete for their eight seconds of glory.

(left)

A capacity crowd fills the Crown Coliseum as fans experience the action-packed excitement of WWE RAW live. With a full calendar of entertainment events, the coliseum regularly attracts tens of thousands of attendees from around the region.

Photo by Greg Foster

(Left to right) Leona O'Berry, Marvin Harrell, Mike Thomas, Hal O'Berry, and Jen Doyle are members of the Cross Creek Cycling Club (C4), a club whose activities go beyond riding bikes. Formed in 2003, the club emphasizes both cycling awareness and community involvement. "Some of our main goals are to make people more aware of cycling, to teach people how to cycle, and to teach them cycling etiquette and the rules of the road," says Leona O'Berry, vice president. "But we also do a lot of charitable work for our community. We're all about giving back to the community through cycling." ★

Design by Gordon Johnson Architecture

CAPE FEAR BOTANICAL GARDEN:
An Urban Oasis

Encompassing seventy-nine acres of pine and hardwood forest, the Garden combines pure, natural beauty with exquisitely designed specialty areas such as the Camellia, Daylily, and Hosta gardens.

Cape Fear Botanical Garden is Fayetteville's front yard. In addition to showcasing nature's beauty, the Garden serves in many roles: environmental stewardship, education and research, the preservation of our agricultural heritage, a unique setting for activities and events, a prime attraction for visitors from near and far and a valuable economic resource for our community.

In 1989, a handful of gardening enthusiasts shared a grand vision. They believed our community should—and could—build a world-class garden in Fayetteville. The group leased a city-owned park, and Cape Fear Botanical Garden had its home. The Garden is less than two miles from the Market House in downtown Fayetteville and overlooks historic Cross Creek and the Cape Fear River. Encompassing seventy-nine acres of pine and hardwood forest, the Garden combines pure, natural beauty with exquisitely designed specialty areas such as the Camellia, Daylily, and Hosta gardens.

Cape Fear Botanical Garden is also the backdrop for educational programs and other special events that contribute to the region's quality of life. For example, the Heritage Garden gives visitors a chance to experience nineteenth-century farm life, complete with an 1886 farmhouse, one-room general store, log corncrib, smokehouse, tobacco barn, and display gardens of herbs and fruit-bearing trees.

The Children's Garden includes the Lilliput Labyrinth, inspired by the classic tale *Gulliver's Travels*, and a Friendship Garden that has plants from six continents. Another important area is the Water Wise Garden sponsored by the Fayetteville Public Works Commission. This area demonstrates water-conserving gardening techniques and displays mulches and plant selections that flourish in hot, dry weather with minimal watering.

Throughout the year, there are tours and classes for all ages and special events including Arbor Day, Spring Plant Sale, the May Day Celebration, Gardener's Garden Tour, Heritage Festival, and the annual Christmas tree recycling program, Grinding of the Greens.

The Garden has been growing ever since its beginning in 1989. Today it is a wonderful reality, but the Garden is not resting on its laurels. Due to continued support and growth, the Garden is ready to embark on the completion of its master plan. The major focus of a new expansion is the construction of the Visitors Pavilion Complex. Encompassing 28,500 square feet, this sprawling center will sit majestically near the entrance of our Garden. The new facility, designed by local firm Gordon Johnson Architecture, will provide year-round space for permanent displays, traveling exhibits, expanded educational programs, meetings, and special events.

Keep watching as the Cape Fear Botanical Garden continues to take root, dig deeper, and grow. ✷

The Visitors Pavilion Complex will allow the Garden to host year-round exhibits and events as well as expand the space for educational programming and meetings.

(left)

Cape Fear Botanical Garden is home to flora and fauna indigenous to the region. Its brilliant grounds showcase the beauty of the area, as seen here at the Gordon Butler Gazebo.

"Many people think Cinco de Mayo is Mexico's independence day, a time to drink beer and party," says Fayetteville resident Julio Cesar Ramirez. But, he points out, the holiday actually commemorates the day in 1862 when four thousand Mexican soldiers began the battle to eventually expel the French from their country. To dispel the common misunderstanding and to promote his native country's heritage, in 2001 Ramirez organized the Cinco de Mayo 10K race. Since then, the event has grown into one of the most popular races of its kind in the country. A USATF-sanctioned event sponsored by the Mexican-American Association Fort Bragg Chapter VII, of which Ramirez is a member, the race attracts runners from around the nation, many of whom stick around to enjoy a host of postrace festivities. ★

All Photos by Alan S. Weiner

*T*HE RACE IS ON!

Photo by Rod Reilly

HOLIDAY INN BORDEAUX:
Offering Hometown Comfort

People stay at hotels for the usual reasons: business and leisure travel. Yet people choose the Holiday Inn Bordeaux in Fayetteville for other important reasons: the homelike comfort, the food, and the hospitality.

The largest hotel in Fayetteville offers all the amenities and services guests would expect from a property of its size, but with the added flavor of hometown friendliness. "It might be cliché, but it really is a home away from home for our guests," says Laura Leal, general manager. It's easy for people to forget they are in a hotel. Guests who return year after year feel like the staff is family, and the staff feel the same. Even the weekly manager's reception is a welcomed way for guests and staff to mingle and unwind.

Central Florida resident James Bayly has been coming to the Holiday Inn Bordeaux every October for years, as part of a family reunion. "Fayetteville is halfway between New York and Florida, where all the relatives are," Bayly says. "We like the fact that the hotel is centrally located and close to the amenities in the surrounding areas, particularly the golf courses, because we come to play golf. But most of all, we love the service we get at the Holiday Inn Bordeaux. From the moment we all check in when the staff greets us by name, to the goody bags they give us, the staff goes

beyond and above what's expected," he says. "We really feel important when we're here."

Recently renovated under new ownership, the Holiday Inn Bordeaux is all about outstanding customer service. "The Holiday Inn Bordeaux has always provided the highest quality in town and the best comfort. That's something we're committed to," says Dipak Thakker, a partner with Aroma Hotels, LLC, new owners of the hotel. "We've spent our energy, time, and approximately two and a half million dollars to improve on the property," he says.

All of the 290 sleeping rooms feature standard amenities for comfort and convenience, including satellite/cable television, high-speed Internet access, telephone, work desk, and coffee/tea maker. The new business wing caters to the business traveler and offers everything one would need to maximize productivity on the road. In addition, as a full-service hotel, the Holiday Inn Bordeaux has a fitness facility open 24/7, two restaurants, and a lounge. Café Bordeaux serves a full hot buffet breakfast every day, as well as a lunch buffet Monday through Friday.

Something else sets the Holiday Inn Bordeaux apart from the others: the convention center. With more than thirty-eight thousand square feet of flexible meeting space, the Holiday Inn Bordeaux is the largest meeting space in the area and can accommodate everything from small meetings to large events, including receptions for up to one thousand people. "With fourteen different meeting rooms, we have a lot of flexibility to host fund-raisers for charities, wedding receptions, corporate meetings, and conventions," says Ramona Moore, director of sales.

For example, every January nearly one thousand Mary Kay consultants from around the East Coast converge on the Holiday Inn Bordeaux for the Annual Jamboree. Pat Fortenberry, national sales director emeritus, has been in charge of planning the event. "The hotel staff does a great job in

(Continued on page 194)

(far left)
Wiley's Grille & Bar offers great food in a friendly and fun atmosphere.

(below)
The Holiday Inn Bordeaux's bright lights and fresh facade are a welcome sight at the end of a long day.

Photo by Greg Foster

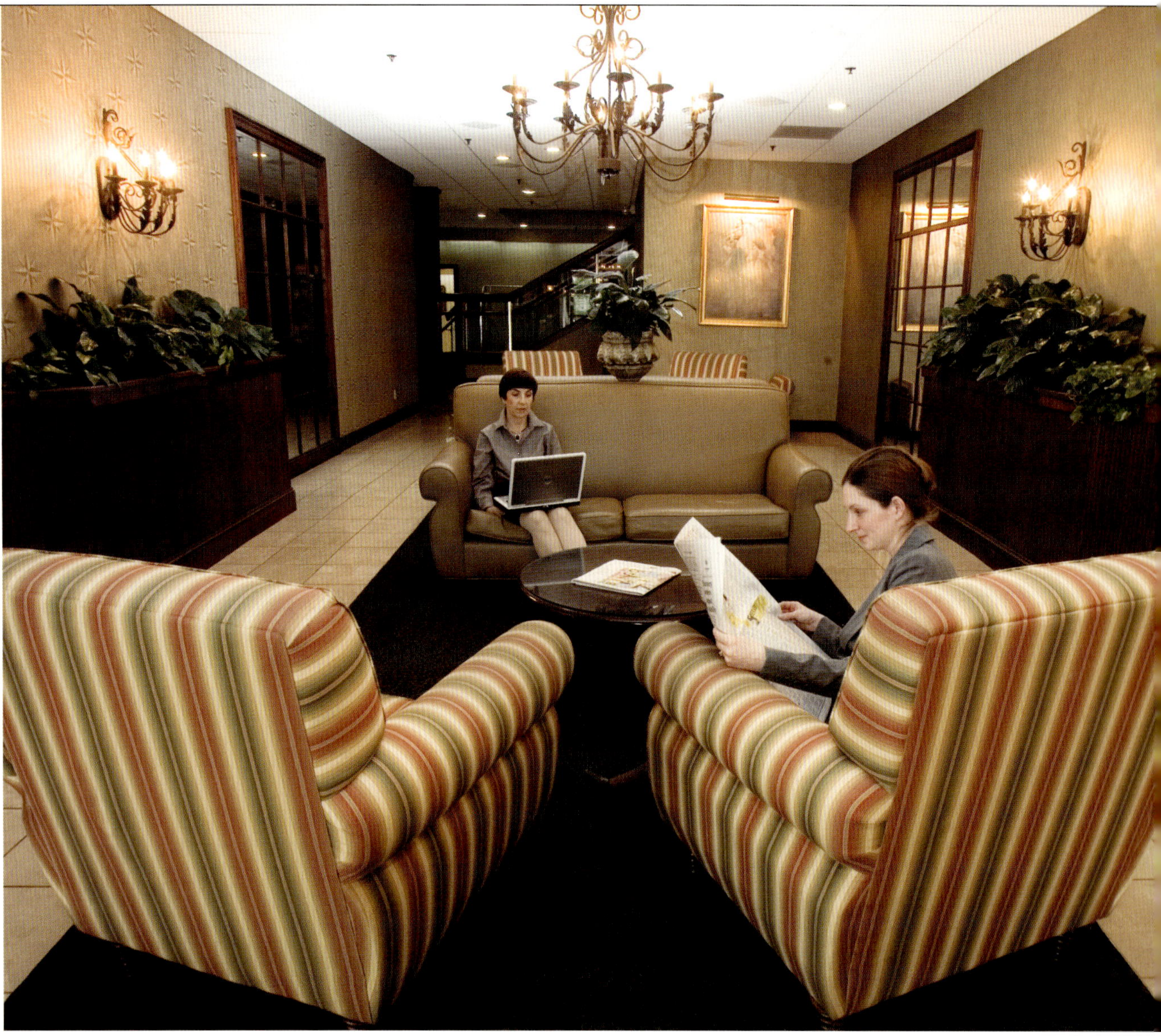

(right)
Many guests prefer to check their email or do some work in the comfort of the lobby. A wireless Internet connection makes it easy.

(below)
With flexible meeting space and the requisite tools, the hotel helps groups power their meetings to a higher level.

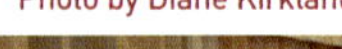

Photo by Diane Kirkland

Photo by Alan S. Weiner

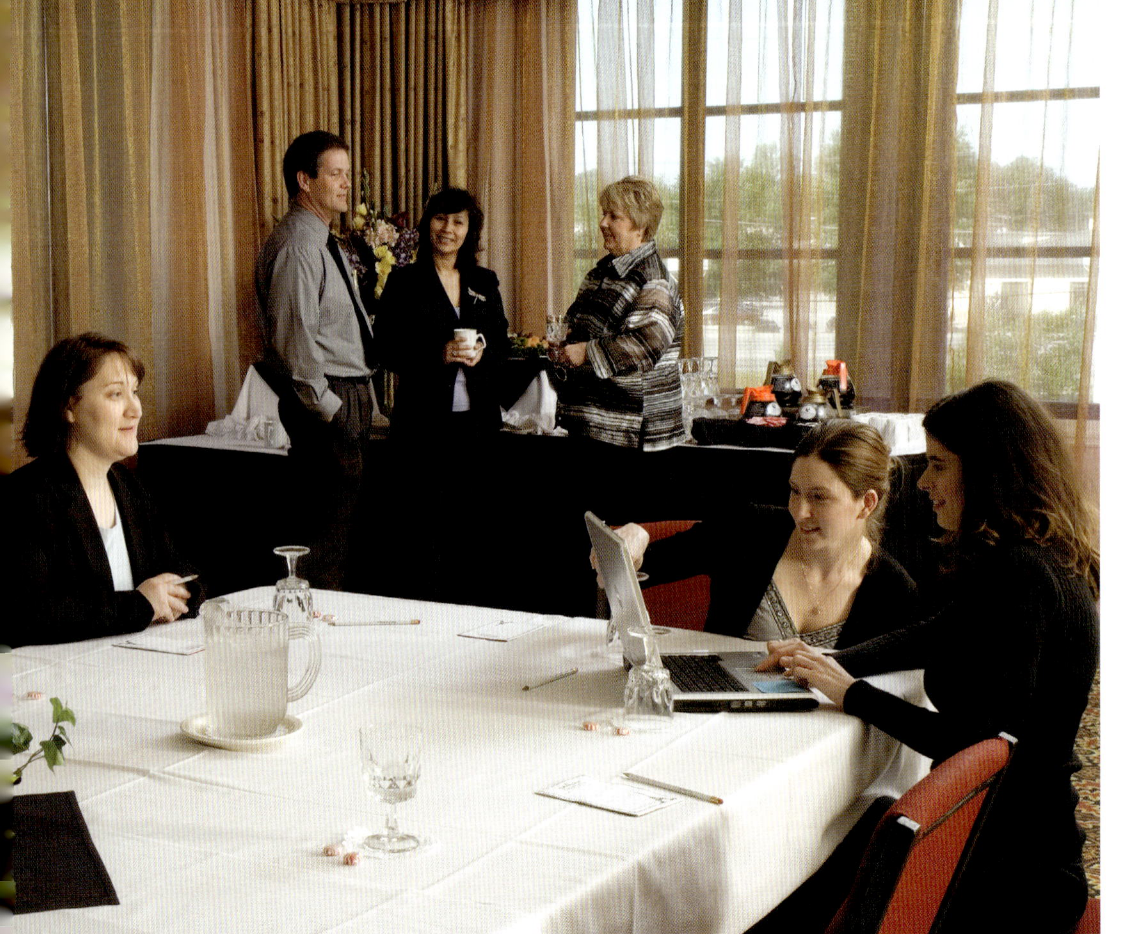

(Holiday Inn Bordeaux continued from page 193)

accommodating all our needs. For instance, we always require a large stage area that we decorate. The staff made sure they were there in plenty of time to help us. They even hung draperies for us," Fortenberry says.

Mary Catherine Moss, director of the Cape Fear Division of the March of Dimes, agrees. For the past several years, the charity has turned to the hotel as the venue for the Signature Chef's Auction. "It's an unusual event featuring about a dozen local chefs who create their signature dishes right on site," she explains. The hotel doesn't skip a beat in setting up all that the culinary masters need for success.

Photo by Diane Kirkland

Whether a home away from home for travelers, or a place to meet, the Holiday Inn Bordeaux aims to please. As Dipak Thakker says, "When people leave this property, they should remember us." ★

Photo by Rod Reilly

(above)
As the largest meeting facility in Fayetteville, the hotel offers elegance on a grand scale for private and corporate events of all types.

(left)
Guests always remark about the family friendly service they receive through the breakfast buffet. The staff enjoys getting to know the guests by name, whether they're here for a couple of days, or return every few weeks.

Each June, graduates from ten high schools in Cumberland County step across the stage and into their futures at their commencement ceremonies. Proud friends and family throughout the area convene at the Crown Center in celebration of an important milestone in their graduates' lives. For more than forty years, the Crown Center has brought the community together and created memorable experiences through quality entertainment. The five-venue complex offers an array of educational and community-based programming, enriching lives and strengthening the community. ✦

All Photos by Bruce R. Feeley

Fayetteville Regional Airport serves the Cape Fear region with connections to the world. For residents of this area, the phrase "Fly Fayetteville" signifies that easy access to daily flights are only a short drive from home. Every year, more than three hundred thousand passengers from a twelve-county area take advantage of daily flights to domestic and international hubs that connect flyers to far-flung destinations. ✫

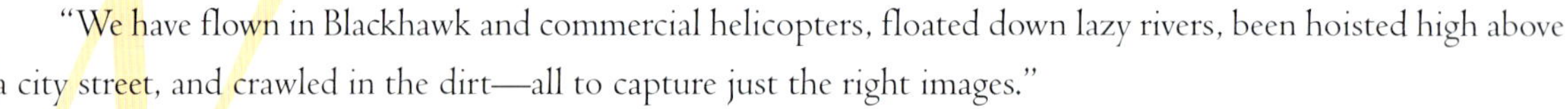

Photo by Bruce R. Feeley

*Founding partners Jan Johnson and Pat Wright
have created hundreds of digital media productions,
earning more than sixty national and international awards.*

MOONLIGHT COMMUNICATIONS INC.
Quality and Creativity

This full-service digital media production company is the company of choice for many businesses and organizations in this region …and beyond.

"We have flown in Blackhawk and commercial helicopters, floated down lazy rivers, been hoisted high above a city street, and crawled in the dirt—all to capture just the right images."

That is the kind of dedication clients expect from Jan Johnson and Pat Wright, founding partners of Moonlight Communications. This full-service digital media production company creates programs from script to screen and everything in between. The partners design, write, light, direct, shoot, and edit.

They started the company in 1993 and have garnered scores of local, national, and international awards for excellence in their field, from Outstanding Woman Entrepreneurs to prestigious Telly Awards, among others.

Moonlight Communications has created videos, DVDs, and Web video for documentary and educational programs, commercials, promotional pieces, and television shows. Their clients include business, industry, government, military, and nonprofit organizations.

Another talent especially appreciated by clients is their ability to deal with sensitive issues and to tactfully interview even the most reluctant subjects . . . all while keeping a close eye on deadlines and budget requirements.

And, if that were not enough, they also saved a historic building on Hay Street, restored it—their office is on the second floor—and received a coveted Carraway Award for historic preservation in North Carolina.

Through production as well as preservation, Moonlight Communications is clearly dedicated to presenting the community's very best image.

There's no doubt about it, Moonlight Communications definitely shines in Fayetteville! ✹

Once home to the New Dixie, Fayetteville's first motion picture theatre, the building that now houses the CAMEO Art House Theatre received the opportunity for a repeat performance in 1998. Three new owners, all with a common interest in art films, building renovation, and downtown renewal, restored the building to its current state-of-the-art film setting. Today, patrons can enjoy an old-time flare for moviegoing while sitting in velvet-covered, cast-iron, opera-style chairs. A separate screening room has also been added with quality projection and sound equipment and stadium-style seats. Recognized by local media as the Coolest Place Downtown, the Best Movie Theatre in Fayetteville, and the Best Place to Take a Date, the CAMEO still exudes nostalgia with the modern perks of wine, imported beer, coffee, or a cappuccino in its lobby/lounge. As Fayetteville's Alternative Cinematic Experience, the CAMEO receives top billing. ★

There she is: Miss Fayetteville Dogwood Festival! For more than a decade, little misses, junior misses, and teens have donned their best smiles and let their personalities shine through to compete for the title of Miss Fayetteville Dogwood Festival. ★

All Photos by Bruce R. Feeley

Photo by Alan S. Weiner

CUMBERLAND COUNTY PUBLIC LIBRARY & INFORMATION CENTER:
The Very Best Place to Start for Learning and Discovery

"The public library has become a popular community meeting place where people come to explore, discuss, read, and learn."

With a mission to educate, enlighten, and entertain, the library provides its customers the best in reading, information, and programs. More than 2 million items are loaned annually, including books, audio books, magazines, CDs, and DVDs. The library's Web site is a portal to the library's catalog as well as to an extensive collection of databases and electronic books. Not only do all library locations offer public computers, but each is also equipped with wireless service.

Professional personnel assist customers with their information needs, whether seeking help with downloading an audio book, researching genealogy, or locating a community resource for a specific topic. The Local & State History Room in the Headquarters Library houses books, maps, pamphlets, newspapers, microfilm, census records, and photographs. What began as a small local history collection now includes extensive material about almost anything concerning North Carolina and Cumberland County.

Programs for all ages—from computer classes and author visits to how-to workshops and poetry slams—fill the library's monthly calendar. Story hours are offered at all locations for birth through fifth grade. Children's programs cover a wide range of topics and formats, including storytelling, puppet shows, creative activities, and performances by musical groups and others.

On the Fourth Friday of every month, the Headquarters Library opens the doors of its large multipurpose room and joins other downtown organizations in participating in Fourth Friday. At its location by Linear Park just down Ray Avenue from Festival Park, Headquarters Library presents local musical groups from various genres for entertaining evenings that are free and open to the public. The events also include refreshments.

Each year the library hosts Summer Reading Clubs for children, teens, and adults. This program, like many others, is supported by the Friends of the Library, a four-hundred-member organization devoted to promoting and supporting library services and programs. The Friends invite authors to speak at the library each month, and annually hold a fund-raiser to support the Library

Endowment Trust. The Friends also accept donated books from the public and conduct quarterly book sales.

"The public library has become a popular community meeting place where people come to explore, discuss, read, and learn in a comfortable and encouraging atmosphere," says library director Jerry Thrasher. "Library staff are here to help our customers navigate the information overload and quickly find just what they need."

The library is looking toward the future, expecting expansion and growth. A new branch is projected in the western part of Cumberland County to meet the demand of an ever-growing population. The library continues to strive to meet the demands for new technology, services, materials, and programs for the county's residents, and to live up to its goal of being "the very best place to start for learning and discovery." ★

(far left)

Each library in the Cumberland County system features a separate children's department where youngsters explore the world through books, music, programs, and computers. Youth services staff members assist children and parents. Library professionals encourage all ages to read and discover.

(below)

In addition to the Headquarters Library in downtown Fayetteville, six branches are located throughout the county. The libraries are popular meeting places for the community and offer a wide range of books, resources, and programs such as author visits, children's story times, and musical performances.

Photo by Rod Reilly

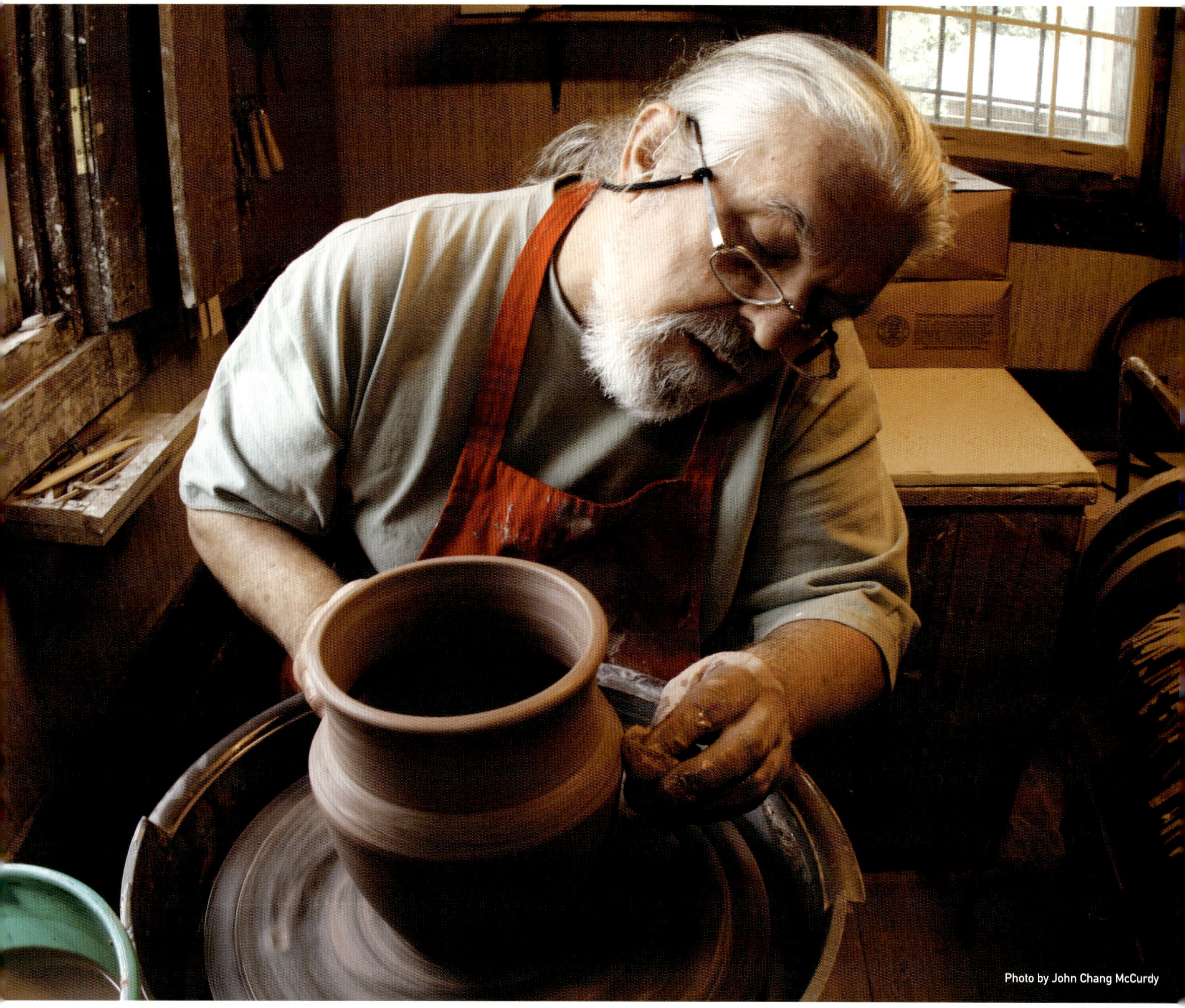

Photo by John Chang McCurdy

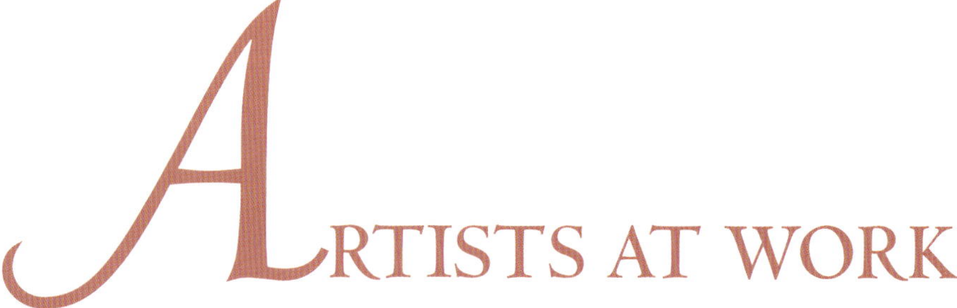

True shoppers are always looking for a new, funky, eclectic place that offers something out of the ordinary. At Greg's downtown you can purchase original watercolor paintings or pottery created by Greg Hathaway or other local artists. Greg does his work in a studio in what used to be an old gristmill. If you're more of a hands-on person, you can paint your own pottery for a unique gift or schedule a birthday party for your child and have a great time making something together. Like any proper gallery, just strolling through the displays can be fun too. ★

ARTISTS AT WORK

Photo by Rod Reilly

Photo by Erin Brethauer

Artist David Goddard knows how to read people. "I really enjoy faces and the nuances of expression," says the young man who has been honing his talent since he was a toddler. "Inspirations for my artwork are usually the subjects themselves. I have an appreciation for the human form and its ability to convey personality and emotion or to evoke an emotional response without a single word." While he is known for his portraits in pencil, acrylic, and oil, many of which have been exhibited in shows throughout the region, Goddard's cultural interests also extend into the realms of theatre, film, and music. ✶

You might say that the president of McCune Technology/Fayetteville Steel has honed his career as a metal fabricator into a fine art. Tree frogs, blue suns, lizards, and lobsters—David McCune creates them all. A professional artist for fifteen years, McCune works in a variety of media but is best known for his metal freestanding sculpture and wall art. From whimsical seaside scenes to solar systems, the pieces, hand-painted and created by McCune, come in a variety of sizes, as evidenced by his largest sculpture, *The Ghost Tower* (pictured here), a replica of the towers of Fayetteville's Confederate Arsenal that was destroyed in the Civil War. Using specialized software for cutting his designs allows McCune to stretch his creative imagination. "I can make a crab the size of a room or the size of an earring," he explained. In addition to homes, offices, restaurants, universities, and historical venues, his unique work is exhibited in twenty-five galleries across the country. ✶

All Photos by Bruce R. Feeley

FAYETTEVILLE REGIONAL AIRPORT:
Soaring to New Heights

Serving a twelve-county area, Fayetteville Regional Airport offers the flights and amenities that make traveling a breeze.

In southeastern North Carolina, travelers know that "Fly Fayetteville" means there is easy access to daily flights within an hour of home. Serving a twelve-county area, Fayetteville Regional Airport offers the flights and amenities that make traveling a breeze.

Every year, some 306,000 passengers pass through Fayetteville Regional Airport, taking advantage of the daily flights to Atlanta, Georgia, and Charlotte, North Carolina. From those cities, travelers can connect to a world of domestic and international flights.

For travelers flying out, Fayetteville Regional provides convenient and affordable twenty-four-hour attended parking. For persons flying into Fayetteville and other North Carolina destinations, there are six national agencies offering rental cars for the trip. And for anyone waiting for a flight in or out, the airport's dining facilities offer great home-cooked breakfast and lunch fare.

Whether coming or going, visitors to the airport will find a freshly rejuvenated, inviting terminal, beautified with new carpet and terrazzo floors, roomier seating, and warm lighting. This interior remake is just the beginning.

Owned and operated by the City of Fayetteville, and guided by an appointed commission, the airport oversees and programs $2.5 million in capital improvement projects. In 2007, a twenty-year, $28 million master plan of improvements was laid out with renovations to include a wider taxiway, rejuvenated runway, reworked perimeter roadway, and upgraded electrical components.

For the aviator, Fayetteville Regional Airport already delivers a full complement of features including a twenty-four-hour, level-three FAA control tower and base radar services; a Category I instrument landing system (CAT I ILS), providing pilots with two hundred feet of vertical guidance and a lateral runway visibility minimum of twenty-six hundred feet; several global positioning system overlays; an on-site Very-High-Frequency Omnidirectional Range (VOR) navigation system; an automated weather observation system; and a 7,708-foot (TODA/TORA) runway capable of handling narrow-body jet aircraft.

Professional Fixed Base Operator services from Landmark Aviation are also available at the airport for general aviation and corporate flyers. In addition to multiple t-hangars for single or light twin aircraft, the airport's general aviation space includes ground lease plats available for the construction of corporate hangars.

Situated just off Interstate 95, halfway between New York City and the state of Florida, Fayetteville is home to nearly two hundred thousand residents, Fort Bragg, and Pope Air Force Base. In its strategic position so near to the base, Fayetteville Regional Airport proudly provides facilities and services for military personnel for training purposes or when the base is undergoing periodic maintenance.

With shorter security lines, flights to key cities, general aviation, a renewed terminal, and planned exterior improvements, Fayetteville Regional Airport is taking North Carolina travelers to new heights. ✶

(far left)
A new conference room in the airport's lower lobby is one of the exciting additions resulting from the terminal remake. The airport commission holds its monthly meetings here.

(below)
For travelers flying out or for those folks meeting arriving passengers, Fayetteville Regional Airport provides convenient, affordable parking close to the terminal.

ROW
7
KELLER WILLIAMS

Anyone from the South knows that an encounter with fire ants means red-hot trouble! Opposing players learned the same about Fayetteville's FireAntz when they claimed the 2007 Southern Professional Hockey League (SPHL) cup. It was the team's first franchise cup and the first championship for Fayetteville in more than a century. Enthusiastic fans are always roused to a fun frenzy by FireAntz mascots, Anthony the Ant and Slapshot the Bear, whose favorite songs are "Who Let the Antz Out?" and "The Bear Necessities." And when team members such as Dylan Row, of Winnipeg, Manitoba, glide into the rink for the starting lineup intro, the fans know that the FireAntz will be serving pure excitement on ice. ★

COURTYARD BY MARRIOTT FAYETTEVILLE:
It's Business as Usual

Picture it: an exhausted business traveler, drained from a long day of meetings, plods through the lobby of the Courtyard by Marriott in Fayetteville. Suit slightly disheveled, tie loosened, and bulging briefcase slung over one shoulder, he trudges into the elevator and makes a beeline to his room, where a hot shower and a plush bed, complete with crisp linens and feather pillows, await him. In the morning, after a good night's sleep, a rested and revitalized traveler, looking refreshed in his stylish and newly pressed ensemble, emerges from the comfort of his well-appointed accommodations, ready to enjoy a hot breakfast and tackle the new day's business dealings with great verve.

This sight is typical at the popular Courtyard by Marriott Fayetteville, where the slogan is "Courtyard by Marriott—Designed by Business Travelers for Business Travelers." According to Christopher Floyd, general manager, while the three-floor, 108-room hotel is perfect for tourists and leisure travelers, several unique features make it ideal for those individuals who find themselves in Fayetteville on business. For starters, the hotel's convenient location, just moments from the city's historic downtown area and Fort Bragg, puts guests in the heart of the city and close to a number of the area's major corporations, affording them the chance to get where they're going quickly while they're in town. In addition, guests can work in the on-site business center, as well as enjoy complimentary high-speed Internet access in each room and free wireless access in all public areas. The hotel also features twenty-four-hour guest services, complimentary parking, a fully equipped exercise room with the opportunity to visit the nearby Gold's Gym, a seasonal outdoor pool and year-round indoor spa, a 650-square-foot meeting space, and a full hot breakfast buffet with health-conscious options.

Furthermore, the Courtyard by Marriott Fayetteville offers the type of outstanding customer service that has become synonymous with the Marriott name. "With this name comes a huge responsibility to uphold the standards of service and quality that Marriott instilled eighty years ago when the first root beer stand was opened by J. W. Marriott along with his wife Alice Marriott," Floyd explains. "The lodging industry has changed dramatically over time, but for the past fifty years since the first Marriott hotel was opened in Washington, DC, we have never lost sight of what our purpose is: to provide lodging for weary travelers who expect next-to-nothing, first-class service."

That service is provided by highly trained staff members who "truly have a passion for what they do," Floyd continues. Many of them have been with the hotel for years, not only showing their dedication to the Courtyard by Marriott Fayetteville and the surrounding community, but also demonstrating their unwavering commitment to making every guest's stay a pleasant and memorable one. And although the staff's enthusiasm for serving guests has not changed, the hotel itself has since its doors first opened in 1991.

The Courtyard by Marriott underwent a major renovation in 2003, during which new carpets were installed throughout the hotel, luxurious new mattresses and bedding packages were added to each room, and new soft goods like sofas, desk chairs, lighting, wall vinyl, drapes, and sheers were incorporated across the property. Not long after the renovation was completed, the hotel

(Continued on page 212)

(far left)

At dusk, the Courtyard Fayetteville is a refreshing sight to the traveler who has spent all day out and about. The aesthetically pleasing exterior of the hotel, as well as its inviting and well-appointed interior, makes guests feel like they've come home.

(below)

The open and spacious lobby offers a warm and welcoming feeling to the weary traveler. With comfortable sitting areas, it's an ideal place to have a brief meeting with colleagues or sit down and enjoy the paper before heading out for the day.

All Photos by John Chang McCurdy

(right)

Guests can take a break from their daily routine and relax in the indoor spa. After a day of traveling or attending business meetings, it's the kind of respite that helps rejuvenate the mind and the body.

(below)

The Courtyard's complimentary high-speed Internet service allows busy travelers to keep up-to-date from the comfort of their room. This kind of convenience makes the hotel perfect for businesspeople who are in town representing a wide array of industries.

All Photos by John Chang McCurdy

(Courtyard by Marriott Fayetteville continued from page 211)

made even more room enhancements, including the new Bathroom Experience, with spa-inspired amenities in every bathroom, and the new Shower Experience, which offers more shower space with curved shower rods and new shower heads that provide more water pressure and enhanced settings.

"Focus on the customer is our number-one priority," Floyd notes. "As times change, so do the needs of our guests. We recognize that there are many types of guests out there, and Courtyard by Marriott listens to their ideas and opinions and strives to answer them."

He adds, "The guest is always right. We wouldn't be in business if we did not believe in such a philosophy."

That customer-centric perspective, coupled with the hotel's many amenities, has made the Courtyard by Marriott Fayetteville the area's leader in meeting travelers' lodging needs. That's just what weary business travelers, like the one who walks through the lobby after a hard day's work heading towards his comfortable and welcoming room, likes to hear. ✸

(below)
Guests can start their day off right with a visit to the Courtyard Cafe, where they can choose from the hotel's popular hot breakfast buffet or from a variety of a la carte items.

Acting Out

The play's the thing at the Gilbert Theater, whether it's a staging of a modern-day social-satire musical like *Doctor! Doctor!* or the timeless Charles Dickens morality tale, *A Christmas Carol*. Founded in 1994 by Lynn Pryer, the Gilbert Theater produces quality contemporary and classical productions, including works by William Shakespeare, Dylan Thomas, Eve Ensler, Moises Kaufman, and Lori Parks. In keeping with its mission to serve a diverse community, the Gilbert Theater has produced a children's puppet show, special performances for nonsighted audiences, staged readings, and theater workshops led by experts in their fields. Support for local artists is provided through a statewide playwriting competition and recognition of outstanding new writers, regular productions of original local/regional plays, student review nights, and rehearsal space for local actors, musicians, and artists. ✸

Lumberton, North Carolina, native Annie Gane *(on floor)* has worked all over the country as a professional actress, but she always loves coming home. In 2007, she shone in the role of Cinderella, one of several special events performances put on by the Cape Fear Regional Theater. The event also included a pre-performance tea party and Cinderella meet-and-greet for young attendees and their parents. Since its first production in 1962, the Cape Fear Regional Theater has built a national reputation as a top professional theater company, bringing together a unique combination of professional and nonprofessional actors, writers, and designers from throughout the state and the nation. To fulfill its mission to entertain, enlighten, and inspire, the theater supports an annual series of plays, performances, and special events for all ages. ★

A look inside one of Beasley Broadcast Group's downtown Fayetteville radio studios.

BEASLEY BROADCAST GROUP:
The Voice of Fayetteville

In Fayetteville alone, Beasley Broadcast Group's holdings include six stations covering a broad spectrum of music hosted by engaging on-air personalities.

Every week, more than a half-million listeners tune in to the Fayetteville radio stations owned by the Beasley Broadcast Group Inc. The company's origins date back to 1961 in nearby Benson, North Carolina, where founder George Beasley invested in his first station. Now Beasley's forty-plus stations in cities like Miami, Philadelphia, Las Vegas, and Augusta, as well as in North Carolina's Coastal and Fayetteville markets, make up the eighteenth-largest radio broadcast company in the nation.

In Fayetteville alone, Beasley Broadcast Group's holdings include six stations covering a broad spectrum of music hosted by engaging on-air personalities. Beasley's stable of market-leading stations includes WKML 95.7 FM, playing "Carolina's Best & Most Country," while WZFX 99.1 FM, known as "The Big Stick—Foxy 99," plays to a younger, urban audience. Other Beasley stations in Fayetteville include WUKS "Kiss 107.7-FM," featuring Urban Adult Contemporary; WFLB "96.5 The Drive," playing Classic Hits; WAZZ 1490 AM, with musical memories of the '50s, '60s, and '70s; and WTEL 1160 AM, offering religious programming.

In addition to entertaining formats and exciting prize promotions, community involvement is another vital element of Beasley Broadcast Group. While the airways are often used to raise funds or awareness for community needs, Beasley personnel, most of whom are longtime, well-known Fayetteville residents, regularly participate in civic endeavors. They take pride in representing Beasley stations while lending a hand and a voice to the needs of the United Way, March of Dimes, Autism Society, Salvation Army, St. Jude Children's Hospital, and a host of other charitable and educational organizations. ✸

Every culture has them. The earliest recorded history can be traced to 3400 B.C. They have gone from being the property of the very wealthy to an item found at every economic level. They are practical, decorative, and fun. In the past thirty years there has been a revival in what used to be called quilting bees. Today, hundreds of quilting clubs, like the Tarheel Quilters Guild that meets at the Westminster Presbyterian Church in Fayetteville, are creating new and old designs. Thimbles, which are essential to the quilt-making process, have a parallel history. They have been made of bronze, leather, rubber, glass, whale bone, ivory, wood, mother of pearl, and various metals. Some have even been decorated with diamonds, sapphires, and rubies. ✹

All Photos by Bruce R. Feeley

HINKAMP JEWELERS:
The Genuine Article

"Just like our parents, we sell the finest jewelry, give customers a fair price, and attend to every detail of customer service."

From the long family history in Fayetteville to the fine jewelry they sell, Hinkamp Jewelers is the genuine article. In a world of impersonal mega-stores, Hinkamp's is a family-owned business. David and Walter B. (Wally) Hinkamp Jr. were born and raised in Fayetteville and grew up in the jewelry business working with their parents. "They were dedicated to exceptional personal service, and we carry on that tradition right down to our signature gold foil paper, free gift wrap, and hand-made bows," said David Hinkamp.

Longtime Fayetteville residents may remember the Jewel Box. Walter B. Hinkamp Sr., Robert Tyndall, and the future Mrs. Walter Hinkamp all worked there. In 1955, Hinkamp and Tyndall became partners and opened Tyndall's Jewelers. Nineteen years later, Tyndall retired, Hinkamp bought out his share, and Hinkamp Jewelers was established.

"Just like our parents, we sell the finest jewelry, give customers a fair price, and attend to every detail of customer service, including checking and cleaning their jewelry for free. Another free service is our knowledge."

Both Wally and Carrie Lambert are graduates of the Gemological Institute of America, trained in grading diamonds and colored stones. Willie Dorman has forty years experience in the industry. Gary See-Wai has twenty-five years experience as a bench jeweler. David specializes in sales and is a graduate of the Holland School for Jewelers. Wally is a past president of the North Carolina Jewelers' Association, assuming the presidency again in 2008.

"We're glad to share what we know. One reason we're still here—and serving a second generation of our parents' customers—is that people trust us. They come because of our service or because a friend or family member recommended us."

Hinkamp Jewelers does a lot of custom work based on a customer's idea or creating an idea for a unique design. "We're always striving to bring the best to our customers, and that's why we're the exclusive dealer in Fayetteville for Hearts on Fire Diamonds."

A diamond's cut determines how brilliantly it will shine. Less than 1 percent of the world's rough diamonds are pure enough to become Hearts on Fire, and only a select group of artisans worldwide have mastered the skills to cut these gems to the standards that Hearts on Fire sets.

Hinkamp Jewelers is also the exclusive Fayetteville dealer for D-oro, Charles Stern, Galatea diamonds and pearls, and many other unique manufacturers.

Throughout their history, Hinkamp Jewelers has supported the Fayetteville community. "Rather than sponsoring one or two events, we serve on boards and support a number of good causes," David Hinkamp explains.

"My wife Dorothy, our two children Brice and Brett, and Wally's wife Susan, and their son Dawson, think Fayetteville is a great place to live. We're actively involved in our local churches, and our children go to Village Christian Academy. We hope the Hinkamp family tradition of excellence will continue well into the future." ✦

(far left)
In a world of impersonal mega-stores, it's a pleasure to find a business like Hinkamp Jewelers, where customer service and attention to detail come first. Wally Hinkamp Jr. spends time helping a customer select just the right Hearts of Fire diamond tennis bracelet.

(below)
In addition to the fine jewelry customers have come to expect from Hinkamp Jewelers, they know they will always be greeted warmly in this family-owned business. Both Walter B. (Wally) Jr. (left) and David Hinkamp were born and raised in Fayetteville and grew up in the jewelry business.

All Photos by Erin Brethauer

What started in 1998 as a way to build unity and camaraderie among the soldiers and families of the Ninety-sixth Civil Affairs Battalion Family Readiness Group has grown into an annual tradition at Fort Bragg. Every year, hundreds of runners are drawn to the Around the World Run, which features 5K and 10K races for youth and adults. These days, the run is followed by a Cultural Expo, which includes dances, food, music, and displays from countries around the globe. ✴

Photo by Rod Reilly

LAFAYETTE FORD:
Where Community Comes First

Price prefers to focus on the local community that LaFayette Ford has called home since its establishment in 1949.

When Don Price, owner of LaFayette Ford, talks about his business, he rarely mentions cars. In fact, the conversation typically is devoid of topics like the family-owned dealership's outstanding inventory of quality, American-made Ford cars and trucks or the fact that the company has one of the highest percentages of repeat customers in the industry. Instead, Price prefers to focus on the local community that LaFayette Ford has called home since its establishment in 1949.

"If you look after the community, then the community will look after you. That's the idea I've tried to instill here over the years," says Price, who began his automotive career at LaFayette Ford in 1965 after he completed his service in the U.S. Air Force. He started as a salesman; by 1980, he had worked his way up to general sales manager. In 1989, he bought into LaFayette Ford and became dealer principal, and in 1996 he completed the purchase. And while his leadership brought growth and change to the company, Price upheld the community-minded business philosophy that his predecessor, George Purvis, adhered to while he was at the helm. "It's not all about selling cars," Price continues. "You have to be visible and involved and recognize the needs of the community."

For Price and his team of one hundred employees, it all starts with supporting the military bases in Fayetteville, from Fort Bragg to Pope Air Force Base.

"Fayetteville would not have survived or thrived without the military bases in town," he observes. "And those men and women put their lives on the line to protect the freedoms that the businesses and families in Fayetteville have. We should give something back to them." So, in addition to Price formerly serving as chairman of the Military Affairs Council, he also volunteers his time for many special projects that are important to the welfare of the soldiers, airmen and women, and their families. He feels that it's one way of showing his appreciation for the military community.

LaFayette Ford is also very involved in a variety of projects for the Cumberland County school system and other child-centric organizations. For instance, the dealership awards several one-thousand-dollar scholarships each year to outstanding FFA students. It also provides a one-year lease on a new Ford to the Principal of the Year and participates in fund-raising efforts through the Kiwanis Club. "We have to care for our children. They are our future," Price notes.

Looking to the future is something Price is doing in his industry and his business as well. To support the automotive industry and stay abreast of the market on the corporate level, he has served on many Ford-related councils and committees. He was elected by his fellow dealers to positions on Ford's National Dealer Council for North

(Continued on page 224)

(far left)

LaFayette Ford sponsored Fred Lorenzen's #28 stock car during the 1960s. The image has been an enduring legacy for the dealership, which has gone on to sponsor several other NASCAR drivers, including John Andretti, Jeff Burton, Jeremy Mayfield, Sterling Marlin, and Dick Trickle.

(middle left)

Don Price presents local soldier Albert L. Taylor Jr. with the keys to his new Mustang. Providing local servicemen and women with vehicles is just one way for Price and his team to show their support of and appreciation to the people who serve America so proudly.

(left)

The state-of-the-art service facility features commercial truck repair, heavy-duty lifts, and the latest technology. LaFayette Ford can service vehicles ranging from small cars to motor homes.

(LaFayette Ford continued from page 222)

Carolina and South Carolina and the Carolina Ford Dealers Advertising Committee.

Within his own company, he has found ways to enhance LaFayette Ford's already impeccable service. In 2004, the dealership opened a new state-of-the-art sales facility, which is designed to make employees and customers alike proud. It also brings the sales side of the company up to par with the service side, which has always been a number-one concern for Price. In fact, the department now boasts a new Quick Lane, a one-stop convenience service facility for customers to get everything from tires to batteries to brakes and more. "We believe the joy of a good deal is gone after day one," he asserts. "What we have to focus on then is what kind of service we're going to give, and it has to be first class from sale to trade-in."

Now joined by his son-in-law Mark Fisher, who serves as vice president, general manager, and partner, as well as his son Tim Price, also a partner and vice president, Don Price takes care of his customers like he takes care of his employees. With an open-door policy, he strives to be a proactive, hands-on force for the company, tackling problems head-on and always being available to those who work for him and those he serves. His efforts were rewarded in 2004 when Methodist University named him Businessperson of the Year. "It was one of the greatest honors I've ever received," Price explains.

And the business ideology that brought him to that achievement is something he hopes to share with the family members who join LaFayette Ford in the years to come. His grandson is already talking about the car business, so it looks like Price's—and LaFayette Ford's—legacy will live on. "LaFayette Ford is a local, family-owned business," he says. "That's how it's always been, and that's how it'll always be." ★

(far top and bottom left)
LaFayette Ford is a proud sponsor of the annual Classic Car Show, held each year at the Fayetteville Dogwood Festival.

(below)
The Don Price family with their 1949 Ford convertible. (Back row, left to right) Mark and Kim Fisher, Don and Karen Price, Karen and Tim Price; (in car) Drew Price, Addison Fisher, Cayley Fisher, and Ashley Price.

All Photos by Alan S. Weiner

Photo by Alan S. Weiner

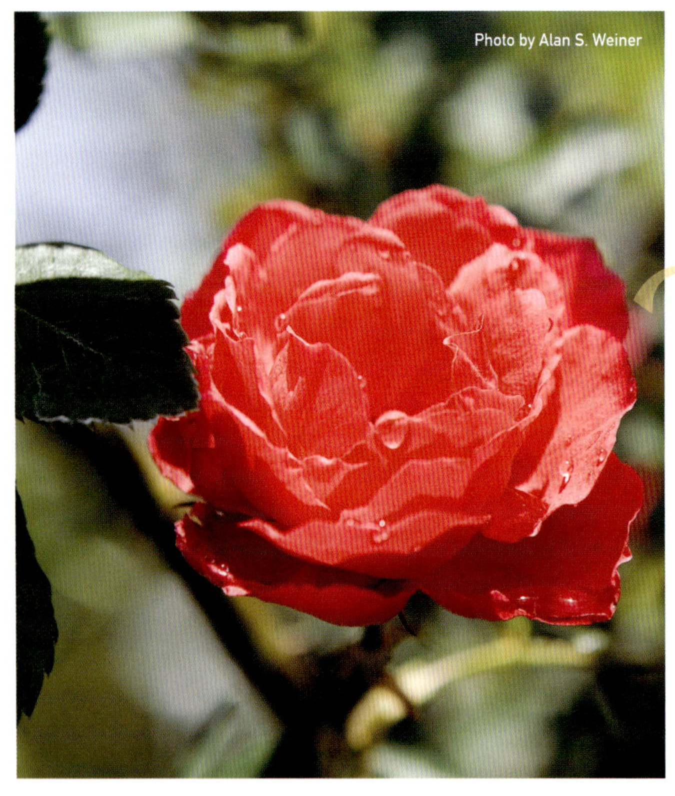

We're all told that one of the best ways to reduce stress is to stop and smell the roses—and one of the nicest places to do that is the Fayetteville Rose Garden located on the campus of Fayetteville Technical Community College. From the middle of May until well into October, this small garden is a mass of fragrant blooms. The Fayetteville Rose Society established the garden in the early 1970s, and the beds showcase more than thirty-five types and approximately one thousand bushes. ✯

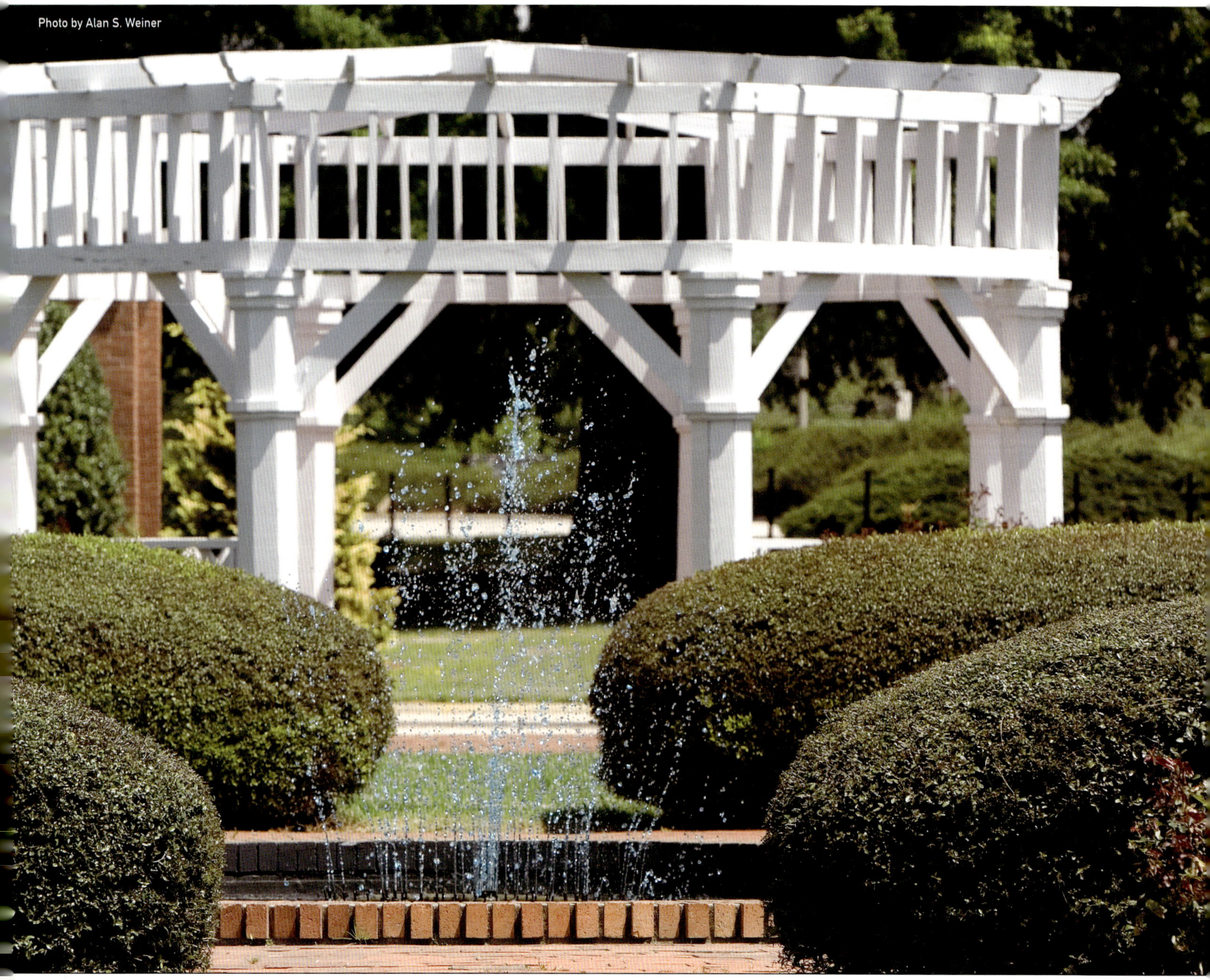

Photo by Alan S. Weiner

A young naturalist-in-training explores the pond in the Lilliput Labyrinth Children's Garden at Cape Fear Botanical Garden. The garden offers educational programs for all ages, from prekindergarten to seniors. There are guided walking tours, hands-on projects, workshops, crafts, and even Cape Fear Kids Summer Day Camp. ✷

Photo by Erin Brethauer

Photo by Bruce R. Feeley

Deanne Wheeler (left) discusses gift options with Diane Young at Holmes Fine Gifts. In addition to gifts for all occasions, Holmes also offers customers a bridal registry and free gift wrapping.

HOLMES FINE GIFTS:
Gifts of a Lifetime

"Some of our customers are from families that have been shopping with us for four generations," said Deanne Wheeler, manager of Holmes Fine Gifts. As part of Holmes Electric Inc., the gift shop was founded in 1908. "Back then they carried electrical products, hardware, and small appliances; it was more like a general/hardware store."

Holmes Fine Gifts is still in the same building on Hay Street downtown. With over five thousand square feet of showroom space, it is one of the largest independent gift stores in North Carolina.

"We've seen downtown go through many changes, and as a member of the Downtown Alliance it's exciting to be part of the revitalization that's going on now." Customers—many of whom have discovered or rediscovered downtown because of the Fourth Friday celebrations—know Holmes is the place for special gifts.

Popular items include Byers' Choice Carolers, ACC collegiate novelties, and fairies by Mark Roberts. "We like to support North Carolina talent such as local artist Hal Broadfoot, and companies like Gap Creek Candles and Artichoke Kitchen," said Wheeler.

Customers find holiday items like Santas, angels, Cuthbertson Christmas china, and Fontanini Heirloom nativity sculptures available year-round. "We work hard to keep up with the latest trends, like monogramming. Our new computerized embroidering machine allows us to personalize gifts for customers."

Throughout its history, Holmes Fine Gifts has supported schools, churches, and other Fayetteville organizations by donating time, money, and merchandise.

"From traditional gifts to whimsical items, we try to carry something for everyone," said Wheeler. Drop by and become part of the Fayetteville tradition of shopping at Holmes Fine Gifts. ✳

"From traditional gifts to whimsical items, we try to carry something for everyone."

While the saying goes that a soldier's work is never done, the Army MWR understands that the men and women who work to defend this country need balance and downtime with their families so they can remain focused and productive. That's why the organization ensures that Fort Bragg offers a wide variety of family-friendly recreational programs throughout the year, allowing military personnel, their spouses, and their children to have important quality time together. Pictured here, Fort Bragg families enjoy the Fort Bragg Fair, an eighteen-day festival held each May that offers a complete amusement park experience, with rides, games, fun foods, a rapelling tower, a jump tower, and much more. This annual event, which also features bands playing everything from Latino and rock to blues and country music, is one of the most highly anticipated and entertaining functions of the year, as evidenced by Blake Bradford and Natalea McGhee, who take their turns on the rapelling and jump towers. In addition to giving little ones and their parents the chance to kick back and have a good time, the fair is a way for Fort Bragg to thank the brave people who dedicate their lives to the well-being of their fellow Americans and citizens around the world. It's something the Army MWR has strived to do since its founding following World War I. Over the years, the organization may have changed in structure, but the core mission has remained the same: to provide "the same quality of life as is afforded the society they are pledged to defend." ★

Photo by Alan S. Weiner

Photo by Alan S. Weiner

Photo by Alan S. Weiner

Photo by John Chang McCurdy

Fort Bragg is known as the Home of the Airborne and Special Operations Forces, but unless you are a Fayetteville resident you probably wouldn't think of it as the home of the only year-round, public ice-skating rink within a sixty-mile radius of the city. Cleland Ice Rink on Reilly Street has an overall skating program that includes open skating, group and private lessons, figure skating clubs, and parties for schools, units, and special-interest groups. Skating is great family fun, kids love having birthday parties there, and adult and youth hockey leagues are available. The rink is easily accessible for military and civilian guests. ✶

Kids everywhere get a kick out of having a ball, and these youngsters are clearly doing both at the Jordan Soccer Complex, home of the Fayetteville Soccer Club (FSC). The multiple fields of the Jordan Complex are designed specifically for soccer games and tournaments and serve as the try-out and practice grounds for Fayetteville's approximately twenty travel teams. With plenty of room on the sidelines for fans, the grounds also include restrooms, a concession stand, and plenty of paved parking spaces. The FSC runs a youth recreational league for players from four to seventeen years of age, an adult league, and a travel team. Soccer is now the most popular and rapidly growing recreational sport in America for girls and boys and has been for the past twenty-five years. In fact, America has more official players—some 18 million—than any other country. ✶

At Gray's Creek Recreation Center, even the youngest tykes can learn self-defense and discipline through karate. The family-oriented class, for beginners as young as age four, is just one example of the many programs offered by Fayetteville-Cumberland Parks and Recreation. The department oversees more than a dozen such recreation centers throughout its park system, offering everything from camps and league sports to classes and outdoor activities to programs specifically for youth or seniors. ✶

THE FAYETTEVILLE OBSERVER:
Documenting History As It Happens Every Day

When you pick up a copy of *The Fayetteville Observer*, you're holding a piece of Tar Heel history. That's because the *Observer*, established in 1816, is North Carolina's oldest newspaper still being published.

But the *Observer* isn't resting on its nearly two-centuries-long track record. The newspaper continues to evolve to meet the needs of its thousands of readers and advertisers in Cumberland and surrounding counties of the Cape Fear region.

What are the results of these changes? Again, check out a typical daily edition. In recent years, the *Observer* has ranked among the top-fifty newspapers in the world for color printing quality, according to judges in an international competition. Closer to home, in journalism circles, the *Observer* has placed number-one for General Excellence among North Carolina's largest newspapers, according to the North Carolina Press Association.

The *Observer* is one of the nation's largest independent daily newspapers. It's also a hometown institution, locally owned by the Fayetteville Publishing Company since 1923. The company is one of Cumberland County's major private employers, with more than four hundred staff members working day and night, 365 days a year, to serve the community.

It's not just an ink-on-paper operation, either. The *Observer* reaches a wide-ranging audience through its award-winning Web site, FayObserver.com, and other Internet-based products.

The newspaper's mission is to tell the story of the community, much as it has since 1816. These days, that mission can involve international assignments, as *Observer* reporters and photographers cover troops from Fort Bragg and Pope Air Force Base while on wartime deployments.

You can learn more about the newspaper's role by visiting its offices at 458 Whitfield Street in Massey Hill. A museum-quality display in the front lobby traces its history, including the *Observer*'s destruction by General William T. Sherman's troops at the end of the Civil War, the newspaper's coverage of this booming military town during World War II, and on up through the latest breaking news. It's a virtual reporter's notebook filled with deadlines, headlines, and daily drama.

Over the years, Fayetteville Publishing Company has branched out from its flagship newspaper. The company publishes *The Carolina Trader*, *Acento Latino*, *The Sandspur*, *Next! Magazine*, and other products. The company has also published the official weekly newspapers for Fort Bragg and Pope Air Force Base for the past decade. And through its commercial printing division, Fayetteville Publishing distributes publications to other parts of the state and across the Southeast.

Some of the company's growth is attributable to technology, including full-color presses installed in 1999. But people are at the heart of this operation—those who work here, of course, but also the loyal customers who follow along as the newspaper keeps turning the page toward the future. They're the real sources behind *The Fayetteville Observer*'s enduring success story. ★

(far left)

As papers stream overhead on a conveyor in The Fayetteville Observer *press hall, pressman Larry Varner meticulously checks Section A of another daily edition.*

(below)

Reporter Kevin Maurer rides in the back of a Humvee in the mountains of Afghanistan in June 2005. Fayetteville Observer *reporters and photographers have traveled to Afghanistan and Iraq several times since the attacks of September 11, 2001.*

At the Fayetteville Museum of Art, inspiring youngsters through art is an ongoing and enjoyable mission. Programs such as "That's So Funny," highlighting the humor in art; "End of Summer Ice Cream Blowout," creating a delicious work of art; and "We Dig Dinosaurs," a prehistoric art adventure, draw kids to the creative world at an early age. Here, a group of two- to five-year-olds, accompanied by parents such as Jennifer Blanton, with son Jacob, learn to examine artwork with a critical eye during "Art Attack," followed by creating a piece of their own. Originally located in Fayetteville's historic Market House, the museum relocated in 1978 to the first building in the state designed and built as an art museum. The facility includes two galleries, classrooms, studio space, a library, and museum store. The relaxing 5.8-acre grounds and pond provide a soothing venue for strolling, attending art festivals and concerts, and viewing the outdoor sculptures. *

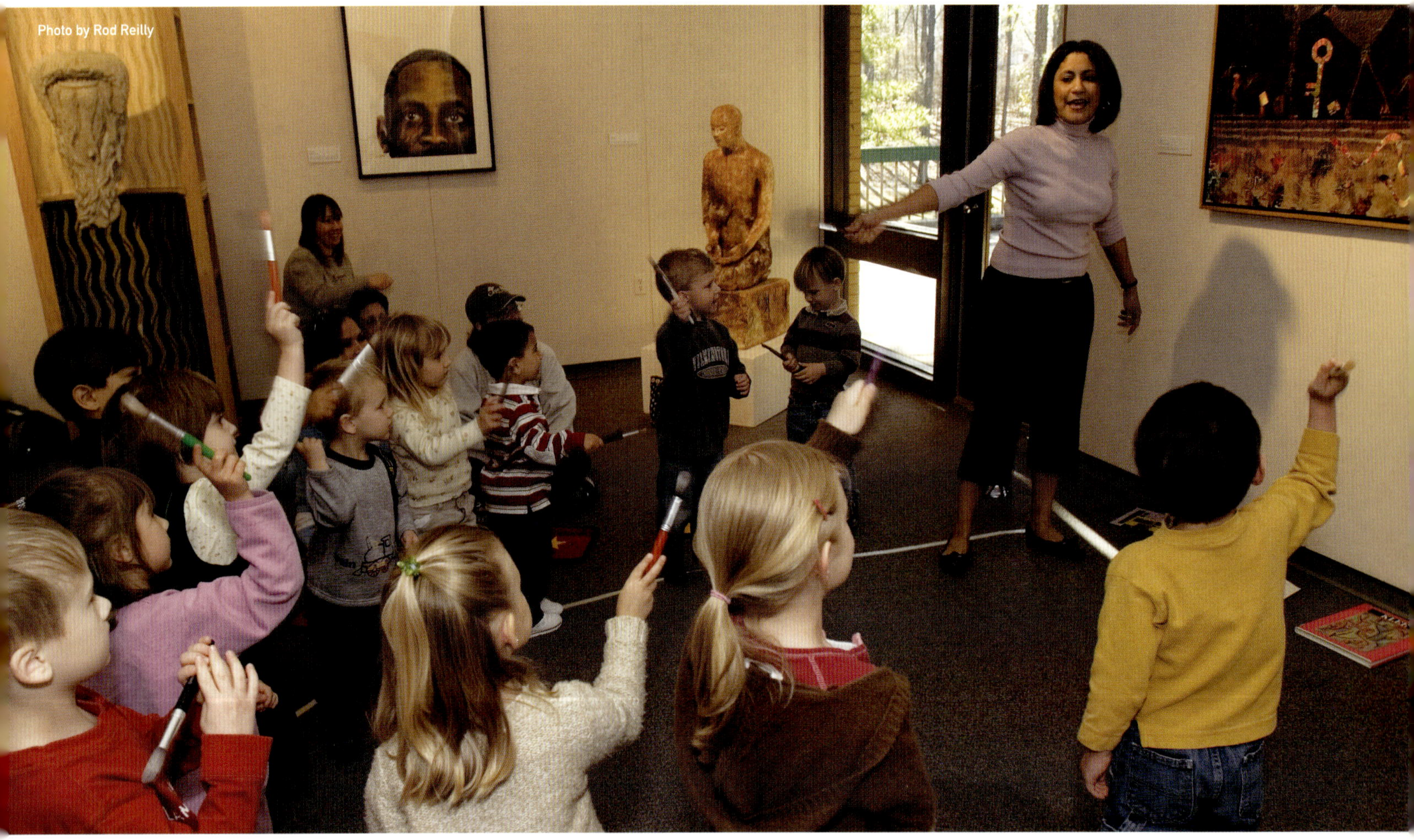
Photo by Rod Reilly

Photo by Rod Reilly

Photo by Rod Reilly

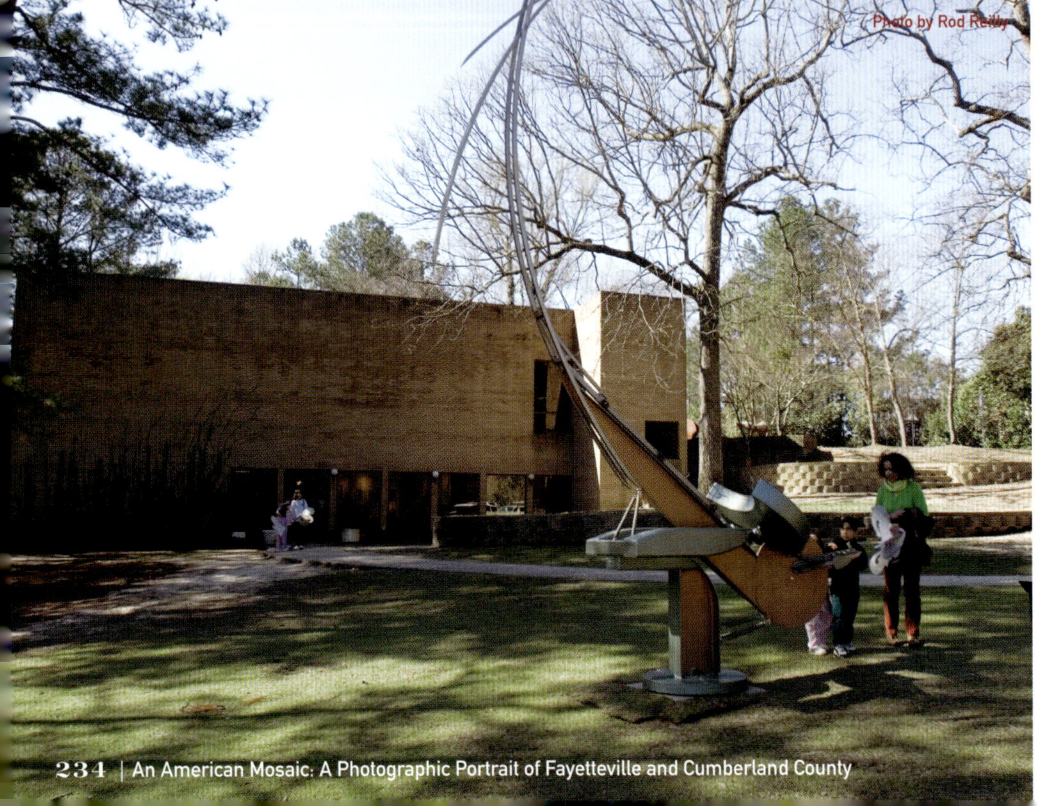

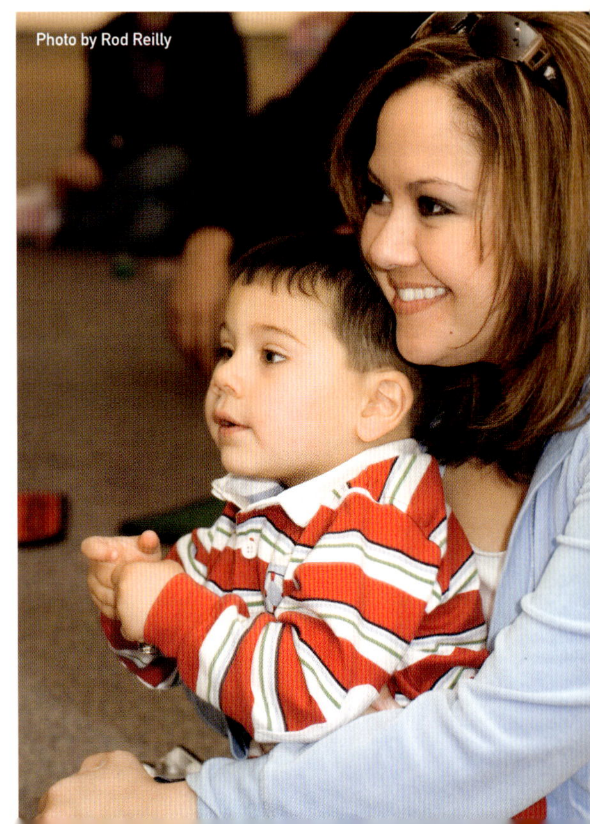

Photo by Alan S. Weiner

Photo by Alan S. Weiner

Photo by Alan S. Weiner

In May 2006, thirteen-year-old Robert Ellis of Fayetteville asked the Fayetteville Motor Speedway officials if he could race the car his stepdad had bought for him. They gave him the go-ahead. After all, the sport is in his family. His stepdad has raced his entire life, and even Ellis's mother enjoys a spin now and then. As the youngest driver ever at the Fayetteville Motor Speedway, Ellis has since moved up to race Open Wheel Modified cars. As he hones his abilities, Ellis also keeps up with his schoolwork (his favorite subject is algebra) and makes time for another extracurricular activity: baseball. But his first love is racing, and a NASCAR career is his ultimate goal. "There's nothing like it," he says. "The rush and excitement. It's a feeling you can't get anywhere else." Races take place at the dirt track speedway every Saturday night April through October. In addition to Open Wheel Modified, the track also hosts Super Late Model, Late Model, Pure Stock, Super Street, and U-Car events. ✸

"We feed a lot of families, support families, and we are a family."

FAMILY FOODS INC.:
We Love Serving You

Occasionally, someone reprimands Ron Matthews, president of Family Foods Inc. in Fayetteville, North Carolina, for sponsoring local events that feature his competitors. He responds, "This event betters our county and its people, and we are servants of the community." Matthews's love for the people of Cumberland County is also evident in the way his company is managed. "We feed a lot of families, support families, and we are a family," he said, describing employees as well as relatives.

Formerly Taylor Foods, Family Foods, a franchise of Taco Bell and Long John Silvers, has been family-owned since 1971 when the company opened one of the first Taco Bell restaurants in the Southeast. Matthews and his wife, Sharon, purchased her brother's share of the business in 1998. At that point the organization had a group of employees who had worked there, left for college, and returned. His son, daughter, and son-in-law also help run the business, so the name change to Family Foods proved a perfect fit.

"We love serving not just our customers, but our employees," Matthews said. "We want to help people improve their lives." Doing so includes active support of programs for youth, veterans, and military families. Every Christmas the company contributes a tithing percentage of sales to the Salvation Army and participates year-round in activities that benefit Fayetteville's residents. Ron and Sharon, both second-generation natives of Cumberland County, are proud of their heritage. True to their faith, they strive to treat their customers just like family. ✳

The Fayetteville State University Jazz Ensemble performs at the Headquarters Library to kick off its community-wide reading project, the Big Read, which encourages the public to read and discuss books. ✭

Photo by Rod Reilly

Photo by Bruce R. Feeley

On a warm summer night, the bright lights of Kiwanis Park shine down on the action during a dynamic and exciting youth baseball game. This all-American pastime is one of Fayetteville's favorites, with parents coming out to cheer on their little pitchers, batters, and fielders every time they hit the baseball diamond. And whether the youngsters play for Dixie Youth Baseball, Little League Baseball, or the traveling North Carolina Stix baseball team, they always show a great deal of skill and good sportsmanship. With so much talent out there, it wouldn't be surprising if some of the names on the backs of these jerseys end up printed on Major League Baseball jerseys one day in the future. ✶

Fayetteville and Cumberland County
Featured Companies

Beasley Broadcast Group

508 Person Street
Fayetteville, North Carolina 28301
910.486.4114
www.bbgi.com

Communication—Broadcasting (p. 216)

Beasley Broadcast Group owns or operates forty-plus radio stations nationwide that are heard by more than 3.7 million listeners. In Fayetteville, the company operates market-leading stations WZFX, WKML, WUKS, WFLB, WAZZ, and WTEL, broadcasting music, entertainment, and information to a broad spectrum of age groups.

Callahan & Rice Insurance Group, Inc.

129 Franklin Street
Fayetteville, North Carolina 28301
910.484.6171 or 877.484.0900
www.callahanrice.com

Insurance—Full Line (p. 134)

Callahan & Rice Insurance Group Inc. delivers a full line of products including property and casualty insurance, life and health insurance, employee benefits, advanced life underwriting, and retirement planning.

Cape Fear Botanical Garden

536 North Eastern Boulevard
Fayetteville, North Carolina 28301
910-486-0221
www.capefearbg.org

Attraction—Botanical Garden (pp. 188-189)

Located on some of the most dynamic land in the region, Cape Fear Botanical Garden is less than two miles from the Market House in downtown, overlooking historic Cross Creek and the Cape Fear River. Encompassing seventy-nine acres of pine and hardwood forest, the garden combines pure natural beauty with exquisitely designed specialty areas such as the Camellia, Daylily, and Hosta gardens. In addition to being a year-round attraction, it is also an important educational institution.

Cape Fear Valley Health System

1638 Owen Drive
Fayetteville, North Carolina 28304
910.609.4000
www.capefearvalley.com

Health Care (pp. 74-77)

Cape Fear Valley Health System provides specialized health care to the greater Fayetteville area as well as six surrounding counties. It is one of just three hospitals in the state to be ranked in the top 5 percent nationally for overall clinical excellence and patient safety by HealthGrades for 2007.

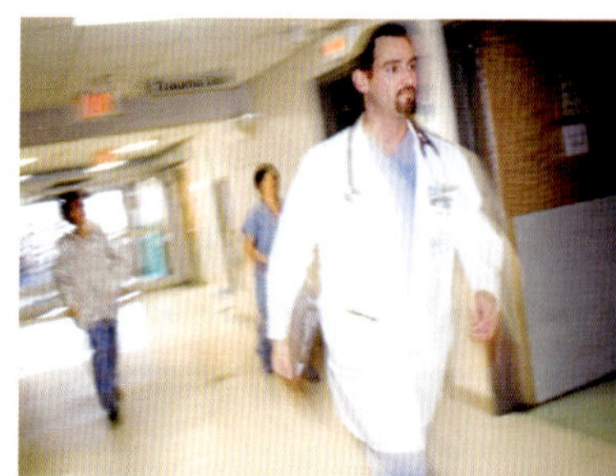

Carolina Mortgage Company

6920 Cliffdale Road
Fayetteville, North Carolina 28314
910.868.4300
www.carolina-mortgage.com

Financial Institution—Mortgage Company (p. 156)

Since 1986, Carolina Mortgage Company in Fayetteville, North Carolina, has waged war on the impersonal service of many financial institutions by tailoring mortgage loans to the individual financial needs of each client. Locally owned and operated, Carolina Mortgage Company promises expedited turnaround on conventional, FHA, and VA loans.

Carpenter, Cammack & Associates

1333 Morganton Road, Suite 202
Fayetteville, North Carolina 28305
910.354.3902
www.ccainsurance.com

Insurance—Property & Casualty (pp. 124-125)

Carpenter, Cammack & Associates, a division of Arthur J. Gallagher, offers medium- and large-sized businesses virtually every major regional commercial property and casualty carrier, including Lloyd's of London and other international markets. The agency has offices in Charlotte, Fayetteville, Raleigh, and Greensboro.

Chamber of Commerce (pp. 68-69)

Through a 2003 merger, the Fayetteville Chamber of Commerce, the Downtown Development Corporation, the Fayetteville Area Economic Development Corporation, and the Small Business Council formed the Cumberland County Business Council, in which each entity does its part "to improve the quality of life by creating wealth, jobs, and investment in our community."

Nonprofit—Library (p. 202-203)

Comprising a Headquarters Library and three regional and three community branches, the Cumberland County Public Library & Information Center is a vital resource for learning and discovery. It loans more than 1.8 million items annually, maintains a Web site portal to the library's catalog and extensive collection of databases and electronic books, and provides educational and entertainment programs for children and adults.

Government—Public School District (pp. 62-65)

The vision of the Cumberland County Schools in Fayetteville, North Carolina, is to become a district of choice, where parents will seek to send their children and students will want to come. With "children first" as the base of all core values, this large system's Governed Choice Program provides students with a variety of learning styles and career options.

Manufacturing Company – Chemicals (pp. 144-145)

DuPont Fayetteville Works is a vital part of the DuPont Company, manufacturing products that improve the safety, health, and standard of living for millions of people around the globe. Opened in 1971 to produce Butacite®, a laminate for safety glass used in the automotive and architectural markets, the facility has expanded exponentially and now manufactures a wide array of well-known products, including Nafion®, Teflon®, SentryGlas®, and Tedlar® resin.

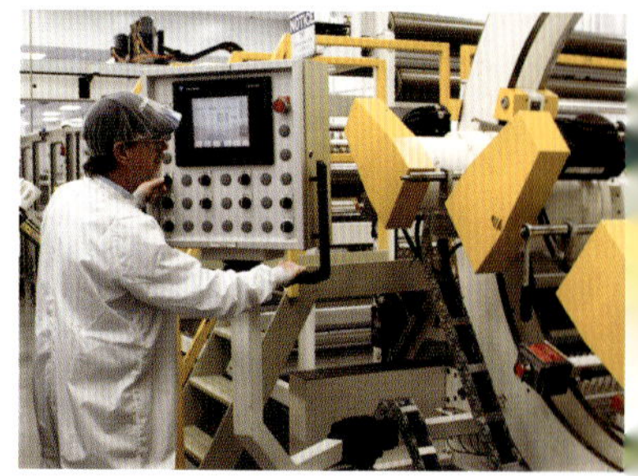

Insurance—Brokerage & Benefits (p. 41)

EbenConcepts is a brokerage company headquartered in Fayetteville with more than twenty offices nationwide. The firm provides employers and employees with unique insurance products and services coupled with exclusive solutions to simplify the benefits administration process.

Builder—Commercial (p. 80)

Established by two of Fayetteville's most experienced real estate and construction professionals, Elmwood Partners excels in building commercial properties that are designed to increase value and ensure client success.

Real Estate—Residential (pp. 168-169)

ERA Pennink & Strother Real Estate was formed in 1999 by the merger of two small real estate firms—one owned by Suzanne Pennink and the other by Larry Strother. In 2001, they purchased an ERA franchise, and today they have more than fifty full-time agents as well as new offices. They are recognized as one of the top companies in the market.

Family Foods Inc.
1046 Bragg Boulevard
Fayetteville, North Carolina 28301
910.323.9700

Restaurant (p. 236)
Family Foods Inc., a franchise of Taco Bell and Long John Silvers, operates ten restaurants in the Cumberland County area. Ron Matthews, president, and his wife Sharon, both natives of Cumberland County, show their devotion to employees, customers, and community by living their motto: "We love serving you."

Fayetteville Area Convention and Visitors Bureau
245 Person Street
Fayetteville, North Carolina 28301
910.483.5311
www.visitfayettevillenc.com

Non-Profit—Convention and Visitors Bureau (pp. 36-37)
This private, nonprofit marketing organization plays a significant role in contributing to the vitality of Cumberland County's tourism industry. The FACVB serves as a vital source of information and event planning, while it also actively shapes the vision, develops the strategy, and implements the most effective programs to position the Fayetteville community as a preferred site for meetings, conventions, and leisure travel.

The Fayetteville Observer
458 Whitfield Street
Fayetteville, North Carolina 28306
910.323.4848
www.fayobserver.com

Communications—Newspaper (pp. 232-233)
The Fayetteville Observer is North Carolina's oldest newspaper still being published, and one of the nation's largest independent dailies. Fayetteville Publishing Company owns the flagship publication and also publishes a number of other newspapers and products.

Fayetteville State University
1200 Murchinson Road
Fayetteville, North Carolina 28301
910.672.1474
www.uncfsu.edu

School—University (pp. 22-25)
Fayetteville State University is a constituent institution of the University of North Carolina. Founded in 1867, it is the oldest historically black public institution of higher learning in North Carolina and currently serves more than sixty-three hundred students. The university is fully accredited by the Southern Association of Colleges and Schools and holds a number of specialized accreditations.

Fayetteville Regional Airport
P.O. Box 64218
Fayetteville, North Carolina 28306
910.433.1160
www.flyfay.com

Regional Airport (pp. 206-207)
Fayetteville Regional Airport serves a twelve-county area, providing daily flights to Atlanta, Georgia, and Charlotte, North Carolina, where travelers can connect to a world of domestic and international flights.

Fayetteville Technical Community College
2201 Hull Road
Fayetteville, North Carolina 28303
910.678.8400
www.faytechcc.edu

School—Community College (pp. 82-83)
Fayetteville Technical Community College offers certificates, diplomas, and associate's degrees in more than one hundred areas of concentration, designed to meet the ever-changing needs of individuals, businesses, and industries. The college also offers off-campus courses and hundreds of online classes. And through its campus-based Center for Business and Industry, FTCC can design specialized training for area employers.

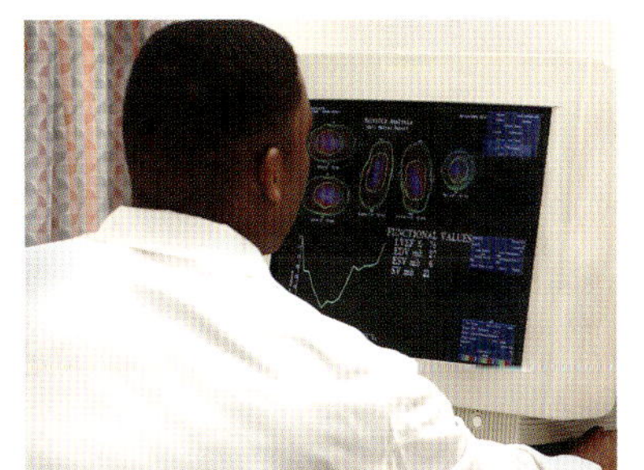

First Citizens Bank
520 Westwood Shopping Center
Fayetteville, North Carolina 28314
910.307.9110
www.firstcitizens.com

Financial Institution—Bank (p. 162)
For more than one hundred years, First Citizens Bank has exemplified its name by putting customers first. Serving the needs of individuals, businesses, professionals, military personnel, and their families throughout Fayetteville and Cumberland County, North Carolina, the bank focuses on forming long-term, viable relationships with every client as well as with the community.

Goodyear Tire & Rubber

5650 Ramsey Street
Fayetteville, North Carolina 28311
910.630.5211
www.goodyear.com

Manufacturing Company—Tires (p. 148)

The Goodyear Fayetteville plant is one of the largest tire manufacturing facilities in the world, with approximately twenty-six hundred employees producing a mixture of passenger, high-performance, and light truck tires. Located on a 403-acre site, the plant is approximately 2.2 million square feet.

H&H Homes Inc.

2919 Breezewood Avenue
Suite 400
Fayetteville, North Carolina 28303
910.486.4864
www.hhhomes.com

Builder—Homes (pp. 96-98)

Building communities with quality, value, and integrity has been the hallmark of this Fayetteville builder since 1991. Owners Ralph and Linda Huff recognize that building a home is a collaboration between everyone involved in the process, from developer to builder to buyer, with the end result being not just a house, but a home.

Hinkamp Jewelers

201 South McPherson Church Road
Fayetteville, North Carolina 28303
910.864.2965

Retail—Jewelry Store (pp. 218-219)

Hinkamp Jewelers is a family-owned business dedicated to selling the finest jewelry, giving customers a fair price, and attending to every detail of customer service, including checking and cleaning their jewelry for free. They are exclusive Fayetteville dealers for Hearts on Fire diamonds, D-oro, Charles Stern, and Galatea diamonds and pearls, and many other unique manufacturers.

Hodges Associates

912 Hay Street
Fayetteville, North Carolina 28305
910.483.8489
www.hodgesassoc.com

Marketing—Public Relations (pp. 158-159)

At Hodges Associates, a full-service marketing, advertising, and public relations agency established in 1974, creativity is more than memorable, attention-grabbing words and compelling design. It's the ability to visualize, develop, and implement unique marketing, branding, and communications strategies that will achieve success for every client and every project.

Holiday Inn Bordeaux

1707 Owen Drive
Fayetteville, North Carolina 28304
910.323.0111
http://hibordeaux.com

Hotel (pp. 192-195)

The Holiday Inn Bordeaux is known in Fayetteville not only as one of the area's largest hotels, but also for its friendly service. The hotel features 290 sleeping rooms, and more than thirty-eight thousand square feet of meeting and convention space.

Holmes Electric Security Systems

127 Hay Street
Fayetteville, North Carolina 28301
910-483-6922
www.holmeselectricsecurity.com

Security Services and Systems (pp. 116-118)

Holmes Electric Security Systems is a family-owned business celebrating its centennial in 2008. It is the only security alarm installation company in southeastern North Carolina that owns and operates its own U.L.-approved central monitoring station. The company serves customers throughout the state from its main office in Fayetteville and its branch office in Wilmington.

Holmes Fine Gifts

127 Hay Street
Fayetteville, North Carolina 28301
910.483.1196
www.homesfinegifts.com

Retail—Gift Shop (p. 228)

As part of Holmes Electric Inc., Holmes Fine Gifts was founded in 1908. The company is still in the same building on Hay Street in downtown Fayetteville. With over five thousand square feet of showroom space, it is one of the largest independent gift stores in North Carolina.

Home Builders Association of Fayetteville Inc.

2935 Breezewood Avenue, Suite 100
Fayetteville, North Carolina 28303
910.826.0648
www.fayhba.org

Nonprofit—Home Builders Association (p. 72)

The Home Builders Association of Fayetteville Inc. (HBA) is a nonprofit organization that is dedicated to bringing awareness to new home construction and promoting affordable housing. Chartered in 1963, the HBA boasts five hundred member companies that not only work to boost Fayetteville's economy, but also build a strong local community.

Hutchens, Senter & Britton, P.A.

4317 Ramsey Street
Fayetteville, North Carolina 28302
910.864.6888
www.hutchensandsenter.com

Law Firm (pp. 128-131)

Based in Fayetteville, Hutchens, Senter & Britton, P.A., is a large law firm dedicated to meeting its local and national clients' needs. The firm's practice areas include creditors' rights, real estate, civil litigation, business and corporate law, catastrophic personal injury, medical malpractice, wrongful death, workers' compensation, as well as services for mediation, arbitration, estates, and condemnation.

Independent Insurance Group Inc.

921 South McPherson Church Road
Fayetteville, North Carolina 28303
910.867.9500
www.iiginc.net

Insurance—Full Line (p. 40)

Committed to delivering the best coverage for individuals and commercial enterprises, Independent Insurance Group Inc. combines extensive knowledge with superb service. Founded by Jim Mozingo in 1992, this agency offers a full range of insurance from reputable carriers in the property and casualty as well as life and health fields.

Jerry Gregory & Associates

2413-3 Robeson Street
Fayetteville, North Carolina 28305
910.486.4900
www.jerrygregory.org

Insurance—Health (p. 164)

Since 1991, Jerry Gregory & Associates, based in Fayetteville, North Carolina, has matched businesses with top-quality health benefit packages from national and international insurance companies. JG&A's unique insurance solutions earn repeated recognition from the National Association of Health Underwriters, and for nine straight years, the company has won the Golden Eagle Award, the highest honor for excellence in the sale of health, dental, and disability income insurance.

LaFayette Ford

5202 Raeford Road
Fayetteville, North Carolina 28304
910.424.0281
www.lafayetteford.com

Retail—Automobile Dealership (pp. 222-225)

LaFayette Ford is among the most successful car dealerships in Fayetteville, boasting one of the highest percentages of repeat customers in the industry. Founded in 1949 and offering an unparalleled selection of quality, American-made Ford cars and trucks, the family-owned business, which has been helmed by Don Price since he purchased the company in 1996, is known for its wide-ranging community service efforts, supporting everything from the military bases in Fayetteville to the Cumberland County school system.

LWSHOMES.com

2919 Breezewood Avenue, Suite 202
Fayetteville, North Carolina 28303
910.482.4663
www.lwshomes.com

Real Estate—Listing Service (pp. 32-33)

LWSHOMES.com is a one-stop shop for new homes in Cumberland and western Harnett counties. With just a click, buyers and REALTORS can choose from multiple floor plans in multiple new-home neighborhoods in a full range of prices.

Methodist University

5400 Ramsey Street
Fayetteville, North Carolina 28311
910-630-7000

School—University (p. 56)

Methodist University provides an undergraduate and graduate education firmly grounded in the liberal arts tradition. It also provides educational and cultural services to the community and prepares students for a variety of careers and educational pursuits. The university has only twenty-two hundred students, more than seventy organizations, and a twelve-to-one student/faculty ratio.

Moonlight Communications Inc.
221 Hay Street
Fayetteville, North Carolina 28301
910.486.9036
www.moonlight1.com

Communication—Video Production (p. 198)
Moonlight Communications Inc. is an award-winning, women-owned digital media production company. They create documentary and educational programs, commercials and promotional pieces, and television shows from script to screen. Their clients represent business, industry, government, and nonprofit groups.

New Century Bank South
2818 Raeford Road
Fayetteville, North Carolina 28303
910.485.5855
www.newcenturybanknc.com

Financial Institution—Banking (pp. 120-121)
New Century Bank South, a subsidiary of New Century Bancorp, is a full-service financial institution based in Fayetteville. Founded as New Century Bank of Fayetteville in June 2003, it now serves approximately eleven thousand customers at six branch locations in Fayetteville, Lumberton, Pembroke, Raeford, and Dublin.

Partnership for Children of Cumberland County
351 Wagoner Drive, Suite 200
Fayetteville, North Carolina 28303
910.867.9700
http://www.ccpfc.org

Nonprofit—Children's Services (pp. 86-89)
The Partnership for Children of Cumberland County (PFC) is the nonprofit organization that brings the public and private sectors together to give children from birth to age five a "Smart Start"—the foundation for a markedly better chance of succeeding in school and ultimately contributing to their community's social and economic future.

Public Works Commission
955 Old Wilmington Road
Fayetteville, North Carolina 28301
910.483.1401
www.faypwc.com

Utility (pp. 100-108)
Since 1905, the Public Works Commission's employees have treated the residents of Fayetteville, North Carolina, not only as valued customers, but also as treasured neighbors. With in-depth involvement in the environment and continuing maintenance and infrastructure upgrades, this utility provides nationally acclaimed electric, water, and sanitary sewer service to the community.

RE/MAX Choice
3709 Raeford Road
Fayetteville, North Carolina 28304
910.483.7500
www.fayettevilledreamhomes.com

Real Estate—Residential (p. 172)
Judy and Rusty Russell, wife and husband, are Broker-Owners of RE/MAX Choice for Fayetteville, North Carolina, and the surrounding counties. As former military brats, they understand the stress of relocating, and as long-term residents, they know the market. As devoted to the community as they are to real estate and each other, these Broker-Owners provide service with integrity.

RLM Communications, Inc.
100 Hay Street, Suite 900
Fayetteville, North Carolina 28301
910.223.1350
www.RLM-Communications.com

Communications (p. 176)
RLM Communications provides critical communications contracting services utilizing leading-edge technology and Commercial Off the Shelf (COTS) equipment. RLM Communications' vast experience and thorough knowledge of tactical and strategic communications assist customers in defining, procuring, and implementing seamless system procurement and integration requirements. Some of the primary areas of focus are secure land, sea, air audio, video, data, and vehicular communications.

Smith Barney
A division of Citigroup Global Markets Inc.
Fayetteville Branch
2153 Valleygate Drive, Suite 201
Fayetteville, North Carolina 28304
910.483.6181 or 800.283.6181
www.smithbarney.com
www.branches.smithbarney.com/
fayettevillenc/

Financial Institution (p. 150)
Smith Barney, the longest continually operating brokerage in Fayetteville and one of the world's largest and most respected financial services firms, provides clients with a comprehensive range of services, from alternative investments and managed money to financial and estate planning and lending strategies.

Team Harris Real Estate

1400 Hope Mills Road
Fayetteville, North Carolina 28304
910.433.2724
www.teamharris.com

Real Estate—Residential (pp. 136-137)

Team Harris Real Estate is a boutique real estate firm serving home buyers and home sellers in the greater Fayetteville area, including military personnel from Fort Bragg. Founded by Jim Harris and now owned by his daughter Wendy Harris, the company offers unparalleled customer service by a team of highly trained real estate professionals, each of whom specializes in an area of the real estate industry.

Tom Keith & Associates

121 South Cool Spring Street
Fayetteville, North Carolina 28301
910.323.3222
www.keithvaluation.com

Real Estate—Appraiser (p. 154)

Established in 1970, this multidisciplinary appraisal firm prepares independent, objective business valuations and real estate appraisals for a variety of clients, including Fortune 500 companies, private firms, government entities, manufacturers, and individual buyers, sellers, and investors.

The University of North Carolina at Pembroke

P.O. Box 1510
Pembroke, North Carolina 28372-1510
800.949.UNCP (8627) or 910.521.6000

School—University (p. 106)

The University of North Carolina at Pembroke offers a personal learning experience with small class sizes and educators dedicated to student success. The university offers forty-four bachelor's and seventeen master's degrees in business, education, liberal arts, and nursing.

About the Publisher

An American Mosaic: A Photographic Portrait of Fayetteville and Cumberland County was published by Bookhouse Group, Inc., under its imprint of Riverbend Books. What many people don't realize is that in addition to picture books on American communities, we also develop and publish institutional histories, commemorative books of all types, contemporary books, and others for clients across the country.

Bookhouse has developed various types of books for prep schools from Utah to Florida, colleges and universities, country clubs, a phone company in Vermont, a church in Atlanta, hospitals, banks, and many other entities. We've also published a catalog for an art collection for a gallery in Texas, a picture book for a worldwide Christian ministry, and a book on a priceless collection of art and antiques for the Atlanta History Center.

These beautiful and treasured tabletop books are developed by our staff as turnkey projects, thus making life easier for the client. If your company has an interest in our publishing services, do not hesitate to contact us.

Founded in 1989, Bookhouse Group is headquartered in a renovated 1920s tobacco warehouse in downtown Atlanta. If you're ever in town, we'd be delighted if you looked us up. Thank you for making possible the publication of **An American Mosaic: A Photographic Portrait of Fayetteville and Cumberland County.**

BOOKHOUSE
GROUP, INC.

Banks ✳ Prep Schools ✳ Hospitals ✳ Insurance Companies ✳
Art Galleries ✳ Museums ✳ Utilities ✳ Country Clubs ✳ Colleges ✳
Churches ✳ Military Academies ✳ Associations

Fayetteville Editorial Team

Kimberly Fox DeMeza, Writer, Roswell, Georgia. Combining business insight with creative flair, DeMeza writes to engage the audience as well as communicate the nuances of the subject matter. While officially beginning her career in public relations in 1980 with a degree in journalism, and following in 1990 with a master's in health management, writing has always been central to her professional experience. From speechwriting to corporate brochures to business magazine feature writing, DeMeza enjoys the process of crafting the message. Delving into the topic is simply one of the benefits, as she believes every writing opportunity is an opportunity to continue to learn.

Rena Distasio, Writer, Tijeras, New Mexico. As a freelance writer, Rena Distasio contributes articles and reviews on a variety of subjects to regional and national publications. She also edits two magazines focused on life in the Four Corners region. In her spare time she and her husband and their dog enjoy the great outdoors from their home in the mountains east of Albuquerque.

Grace Hawthorne, Writer, Atlanta, Georgia. Starting as a reporter, she has written everything from advertising for septic tanks to the libretto for an opera. While in New York, she worked for Time-Life Books and wrote for *Sesame Street*. As a performer, she has appeared at the Carter Presidential Center, Callanwolde Fine Arts Center, and at various corporate functions. Her latest project is a two-woman show called *Pushy Broads and Proper Southern Ladies*.

Amy Meadows, Writer, Canton, Georgia. Meadows is an accomplished feature writer who has been published in a wide variety of local, regional, and national consumer and trade publications since launching her freelance writing career in 2000. She also specializes in producing corporate marketing literature for companies large and small and holds a master's of arts degree in professional writing from Kennesaw State University.

Regina Roths, Writer, Andover, Kansas. Roths has written extensively about business since launching her journalism career in the early 1990s. Her prose can be found in corporate coffee-table books nationwide as well as on regionally produced Web sites, and in print and online magazines, newspapers, and publications. Her love of industry, history, and research gives her a keen insight into writing and communicating a message.

Gail Snyder, Writer, Woodstock, Georgia. Snyder is a writer and editor with twenty years of experience in corporate communications and publishing. She has edited or written articles focusing on corporate management strategies, published articles in a number of trade magazines and journals, and edited both fiction and nonfiction books. Gail enjoys explaining material to an audience in a way that reveals how any subject can be interesting. She earned her bachelor's degree in journalism from Georgia State University, where she went on to complete her master's in communications. Currently she works as a freelance and contract writer and editor.

Erin Brethauer, Photographer, Asheville, North Carolina. Erin believes in engaging photography that tells a story. After graduating from Marquette University in Milwaukee in 2005, Brethauer moved to South Carolina to start her first job as a photographer at *The Morning News* in Florence where she stayed for a year and a half. She is currently a staff photographer at *The Citizen-Times* newspaper in Asheville, North Carolina, where she covers a wide variety of community news. Her work has been nationally recognized.

Bruce R. Feeley, Photographer, Raleigh, North Carolina. Feeley has worked for various news agencies over the past twenty-five years in the Northeast and Southeast. After leaving New York he worked as a staff photographer at Duke University for seven years. He is a regular contributor to *The New York Times*, and his work from the American Dance Festival, in Durham, North Carolina, is in the Local Legacies permanent collection at the Smithsonian in Washington, D.C. His work is primarily editorial and has appeared in *U.S. News & World Report*, *Sports Illustrated*, *USA Today*, and numerous foreign publications. His proudest accomplishment is being a dad to his five-year-old son, Ian James Feeley.

Greg Foster, Photographer, Atlanta, Georgia. For the last twenty years, Greg has produced images for some of the world's leading publications, including *Sports Illustrated*, *Time*, *Fortune*, *ESPN The Magazine*, *Golf Digest*, *USA Weekend*, and *The New York Times*. His corporate clients include The Coca-Cola Company, Norfolk-Southern, HBO, Royal Caribbean, Kodak, and the National Basketball Association. He has also had his photographs featured in the books *The NBA at 50*, *The NBA's Best Shots*, *America 24/7*, and *A Day in the Life of the National Hockey League*. Greg's ongoing personal photography projects include a series of portraits of blues musicians in Texas, Georgia, and the Mississippi Delta, and a series of roadside scenes around the South.

Diane M. Kirkland, Photographer, Atlanta, Georgia. Diane's images have appeared in numerous advertising campaigns, promotional brochures, Web sites, and national and international publications including *Southern Living*, *Time*, *USA Today*, *Lenswork Magazine*, and the *London Times*. She has also been the photographer for two large coffee table books: *Oglethorpe's Dream, A Picture of Georgia* (2001), and *Democracy Restored, A History of the Georgia Capitol* (2007). The Georgia Council for the Arts selected Diane to join their 2007–2008 Touring Artist Rosters, and she was also invited to join the Southern Arts Federation (www.SouthernArtistry.org).

John Chang McCurdy, Photographer, Atlanta, Georgia. McCurdy is a leading photographer on three continents. His works have been exhibited in numerous museums and galleries in the United States and Europe, including the San Francisco Museum of Modern Art. McCurdy was a sole photographer on ten books and contributing photographer on eight books. Novel Prize–winner Halldor Laxness, rector of the University of Edinburgh Magnus Magnusson, and McCurdy worked together on the book *Iceland*. McCurdy was selected as one of the top eight modern masters of fine art photography by Gene Thornton of *The New York Times*.

Rod Reilly, Photographer, Atlanta, Georgia. Since 1979 Reilly has used his training at Carnegie Mellon School of Design and Rochester Institute of Technology to create compelling environmental portraits on location of people as they live and work. His clients include Home Depot, Coca-Cola USA, United Parcel Service, Cox Communications, and McGraw-Hill. Starting his career as a staff shooter for Georgia Pacific, Rod has owned his own studio, Reilly Arts & Letters, for the last twelve years, and travels often on assignment. He is a member of ASMP and the father of three. His work can be seen at rodreillyphoto.com.

Alan S. Weiner, Photographer, Portland, Oregon. Weiner travels extensively both in the United States and abroad. Over the last twenty-three years his work has appeared regularly in *The New York Times*. In addition, his pictures have been published in *USA Today* and in *Time*, *Newsweek*, *Life*, and *People* magazines. He has shot corporate work for IBM, Pepsi, UPS, and other companies large and small. He is also the cofounder of The Wedding Bureau (www.weddingbureau.com). Alan has worked in every region of the country for Riverbend Books. His strengths are in photojournalism.